SUPER TRUCK

NICK BALDWIN

Octopus

**First published in 1981 by
Octopus Books Limited
59 Grosvenor Street London W1**

© 1981 Hennerwood Publications Limited

ISBN 0 7064 1627 9

Produced by Mandarin Publishers Limited
22a Westlands Road Quarry Bay Hong Kong

Printed in Hong Kong

CONTENTS

Endpapers Ottawa half-cab tractors with elevating fifth-wheel couplings unloading oranges at a Kansas soft-drinks factory.

Half-title Custom-painted cab and chromium plated air-cleaner of a Peterbilt 6x4 conventional tractor.

Title spread Top-of-the-range Bedford TM3800 4 x 2 tractor and soft-top semi-trailer for up to 38 tonnes gtw operation.

This spread Kenworth 6 x 4 tractor and low-loader delivering a cement kiln to a works in Bath, Ontario.

THE RISE OF THE BIG RIGS

Although steam-powered carriages first appeared on public roads at the beginning of the 19th century, heavy haulage by steam traction engines began only in the 1860s. Even in those early days weights of up to 50 tons were moved by steam, but this was almost invariably over very short distances. Most road traction engines, in fact, were used for shifting heavy loads, such as large industrial machinery and other equipment, from the factory to the nearest canal or railway yard. That they were not used on longer routes was due mainly to the shortcomings of public roads, which were suitable only for much lighter horse-drawn traffic; moreover, few road bridges of the late 19th century were designed to support weights of more than two or three tons.

Nonetheless, the advantages of steam power over horse power were obvious. Above all, big steam tractors were capable of hauling very heavy indivisible loads. For such work, indeed, they were to remain superior even to most petrol-engined trucks until the 1920s. Until the last years of the 19th century steam traction engines were used for towing trailers. But the Edwardian era saw increasing use of steam wagons — that is, steam-powered trucks designed to carry loads as well as to tow them.

During their heyday in the first decade of the present century probably the greatest concentration of steam wagons in the world was to be found in the industrial north of England. Of more than 30 British manufacturers by far the most successful were Foden and Sentinel. Foden was founded in 1887 at Sandbach, Cheshire (the company's factory is still there) as a builder of steam engines that were used mainly by agricultural contractors and road hauliers. Sentinel, based at Shrewsbury, grew out of a firm of marine engineers that produced its first steam wagon, a 5-tonner, in 1906. Steam wagons were used in France and Germany until World War I. In France an important pioneer among steam trucks was the Amédée Bollée, while the De Dion, Bouton firm was among the earliest to produce both steam- and petrol-powered vehicles in some quantity. Probably the best of the large French steam wagons were built by Purrey, who ceased production only in 1929. Of the great present-day American truckbuilders, White, of Cleveland, Ohio, made its name originally as a builder of steam-powered luxury cars. It produced its

Preceding two pages Typical early 1970s line-up at an American truck-stop. From right: Kenworth, Peterbilt, White, and International cab-over tractors. Cab styling has changed little since then.

Above This 1928 Foden 10/12-ton steam wagon developed a nominal 45 bhp and could make about 32 km/h (20 mph). Note the poor ratio of cab to load space. Foden built its first diesel-engined truck in 1931.

first steamer van in 1901 and progressed to steam-powered wagons of up to 3 tons until it turned exclusively to production of petrol-engined trucks after 1911.

In Britain steam wagons remained widely used for heavy haulage until the 1930s when legislation (inspired, it was widely believed, by pressure from the railways lobby) imposed a tax on the unladen weight of trucks. This proved a particular handicap to steam wagons, which were almost invariably heavier, within each weight category, than their petrol- or diesel-engined counterparts. The new legislation meant effectively that the steam wagon operator had a choice of carrying uneconomic loads or contravening the law by overloading.

The dominance of petrol engines

Although such legislation posed a serious threat to the steam wagon, the prime reason for its demise was, of course, the rapid improvement in the internal-combustion engine fuelled by petrol. This had first been applied to road vehicles in 1885-6 by the Germans Karl Benz and Gottlieb Daimler. Probably the world's first petrol-powered commercial vehicle was the wagonette produced by Panhard et Levassor, of Paris, in 1893. Light trucks built by Benz and Daimler and also by the other great French pioneer, Peugeot, followed in 1894. These vehicles had the advantage over steam wagons of lighter-weight components, a more concentrated fuel, and the ability to start from cold in minutes rather than an hour or more. To begin with, the internal-combustion-engined lorries could carry little more than could the cars from which they were developed. However, in the late 1890s trucks with larger engines, usually with 2 cylinders (deemed adequate for unrefined commercial purposes), took payloads of 1½ or even 2 tons; above that weight all loads on the road were either drawn by horse or carried on 3- or 5-ton steam wagons.

The only competitor to these three forms of motive power was electricity which, for a few years from 1900, looked as though it might prove a formidable rival. This possibility disappeared as soon as the petrol-engined vehicle proved that it could deliver goods swiftly and reliably over ever-increasing distances — something that was beyond the capacity of the electric vehicle, whose batteries needed to be re-charged every few miles. Before long the electric vehicle's only role, like that of the horse and cart, was in local delivery work, where both survived until the 1950s; the electric milk-delivery 'float' remains a familiar sight in urban Britain.

Although Germany and France were first with internal-combustion engines, North America and the rest of Europe were very close behind and in some cases had overtaken the pioneers by about 1910. In Britain the major truck makers, such as Leyland (founded 1896), Thornycroft (1896), Albion (1902), Maudslay (1903), Dennis (1904), Commer (1905), and Karrier (1908) were thriving; in North America Autocar, International, Mack, Reo, and White were operating by 1910.

Some of the early motor firms were primarily car makers; many of the heavy truck firms, on the other hand, entered the industry from some other branch of engineering — often in the agricultural field — and in almost every case had established its production plant in the midst of a manufacturing area where there were plenty of goods to be moved. Traditional haulage firms viewed early motor vehicles with attitudes ranging from suspicion to hostility, but there were a few manufacturers, large stores, and brewers with their own goods to be moved who were keen to reduce the manpower and stabling inseparable from horse transport and who were willing to try the new methods. Finding drivers and mechanics was a problem, but the truck firms could usually provide teachers, drivers, or advice. From very slow beginnings it was obvious by 1906 that the steam- or petrol-powered truck was here to stay.

Mack AC-model military trucks await shipment to Europe in 1918. British soldiers dubbed them *Bulldog* — a name associated with Mack ever since. A similar model, with radiator behind the engine, remained in production until 1938.

Total truck (and bus) production in the United States in 1904 was 700. It had reached the 1,000 mark in 1907, 6,000 in 1910, and 25,000 per year by the outbreak of World War I. Britain had a grand total of 4,000 trucks in use in 1904, but most of these were little more than converted cars. This figure had increased to 30,000 in 1910 and to 132,000 in 1914. Records of vehicle production by category were not kept in Britain until the 1920s, but the total output of private cars and commercial vehicles in 1908 was 10,500 and in 1913, 34,000.

By 1910 virtually all the firms that had simultaneously made vehicles with steam, electric, and petrol engines had switched to the last and were moving upwards in the weight range into the area once served only by steam. The largest petrol-engined standard goods vehicle of the period was the two-axle 10-tonner built from 1909 to 1914 by the Hewitt company of New York. This had forward control (driver over engine), like many of the early vehicles from that country, whereas normal control (seat behind bonnet) was the order of the day in Europe (with one or two notable exceptions like Karrier) and would continue to be until the mid-1930s.

In 1912 Hewitt was absorbed into a consortium which included Mack, and its founder, Edward Hewitt, became chief designer of Mack trucks. The year before had seen the first of the takeovers and mergers which in the United States, as in Europe, would reduce the number of truck manufacturers from hundreds to the few major names today: the firm of GMC was formed by the merger of Rapid, of Detroit, and Reliance, of Owosso, Michigan, which had recently been acquired by General Motors Truck Company, of Pontiac, Michigan.

World War I confirmed manufacturers' faith in the superiority of petrol-engined trucks over steam-powered vehicles, and by the end of 1918 tens of thousands of servicemen had been trained in their use and maintenance. The war also transformed the truck industry on both sides of the Atlantic. European factories, despite vastly increased output, could not cope with the wartime demand, even with several firms making 1,000 or more trucks per year and the largest of all, AEC of Walthamstow (founded 1912), averaging 2,000 per year throughout the war. Before the United States entered the war in 1917 she shipped thousands of trucks to the Allies, and by 1918 was turning out a staggering 250,000 commercial vehicles per year — far in excess of Europe's total.

The inter-war years

High output helped to reduce unit prices and ensured the use of standardised designs with interchangeable parts (a bugbear of the early trucks had been that no two were alike, owing to endless hours of hand fitting of parts). It also gave rise to a components industry, whereas previously manufacturers had made virtually everything they needed (apart from electrical systems and tyres) under their own roof. Henceforward, the North American truck industry would tend to be split between 'makers', such as Mack, and the myriad 'assemblers', who simply bought the best or cheapest components and fitted them together. Obviously the more this happened the greater was the demand for the engines, axles, gearboxes, or whatever that the specialists made. In turn this lowered the unit price of the parts and allowed maximum funds for research and development by the individual specialists, so that some of the 'assembled' trucks became as good as if not better than the 'manufactured' ones. This trend has continued in North America. It is less common in Europe, although in the 1930s the 'assembled' ERF was perhaps the best truck in Britain.

The 1920s saw the gradual refinement of heavy trucks with the adoption of pneumatic tyres, self-starters, servo-assisted brakes on all wheels, enclosed cabs, six-cylinder engines in place of the ubiquitous fours of World War I, electric lighting, and the arrival of six wheelers and articulated trucks. The advantages of mass-production, demonstrated by the prodigious success of Henry Ford's Model T (introduced in 1908), encouraged many car makers to build heavier vehicles than the simple car-derived vans and pickups that had formed their staple commercial products before the war. Amongst the protagonists Ford, beginning with their 3.3-litre A of 1927, as well as Chevrolet, Dodge, and others in America, Citroën in France, and Morris and Rootes (who had acquired Commer) in England, all made increasingly heavy vehicles by car-production methods. Prices fell and the true heavy-truck makers were forced to become more specialised.

Diesel versus petrol

The real division between the car and the truck makers came with the diesel engine, which was adopted rapidly by the quality truck makers after 1930. The principle of compression ignition had been understood by Herbert Akroyd Stuart in Britain and Dr Rudolf Diesel in Germany in the 1890s, but it had not been possible to apply it to road vehicles because of the massive weight required to make the engines strong enough to withstand compression pressures. Diesel had tried unsuccessfully to build a workable truck engine in 1910, and it was not until 1923-4 that his pupils at Benz and MAN (Maschinenfabrik Augsburg-Nürnberg) finally put diesel-engined trucks on the road. They were slow, heavy, and lumbering, but they used cheaper and safer fuel than petrol and did not require the ignition systems that were one of the few items still giving trouble on internal-combustion vehicles. Mercedes-Benz (Daimler and Benz had united in 1926) and the Swiss firm Saurer (founded in 1903) were both making successful diesel trucks by 1928, and they were followed by a host of French, German, Italian, and British makers. The real breakthrough came in Britain in 1929 when both Gardner (an engine specialist) and AEC made diesels that could be run at petrol-engine speeds and, therefore, could be directly interchangeable on vehicles. The Gardner engine was the world's first successfully to employ direct injection instead of the less efficient pre-combustion-chamber method. It became the yardstick by which all others were measured, and indeed it is still regarded as the most fuel-efficient diesel produced. Many British truck firms used Gardner diesels in the 1930s, although the largest, such as Leyland, offered their own designs from 1931.

Petrol had never been as heavily taxed in North America as in Europe and there was, therefore, less incentive to switch from petrol engines to diesels. In 1931, however, Cummins launched a diesel as a replacement unit for worn-out petrol engines on trucks; and within a few years Cummins designs were becoming adopted as original equipment by a few of the 'assemblers'. Other American proprietary engine makers bought European knowhow from experts such as Sir Harry Ricardo. In 1937, however, Mack, the largest manufacturer of heavy-duty quality trucks, introduced its own diesel and gave impetus to what became a switchover to diesels in North America. This was a very gradual process: it was completed on heavy vehicles only in the early 1970s, and is happening only now on middleweights (which have mostly been diesel-powered in Europe since the mid-1950s).

Some 15,000 diesel-powered vehicles were in use in Britain in 1937, and nearly all of these were maximum-capacity trucks and buses. Successive legislation had increased maximum permitted weights, and the rigid eight-wheeler (a truck with four axles) took advantage of this in Britain in the mid-1930s with a gross weight of 22 tons. In North America and the rest of Europe, however, the preference was for either a rigid truck with a drawbar trailer or an articulated truck — that is, a tractor and semi-trailer.

Specialised trucks with all-wheel drive had been developed for off-road use since before World War I, and when such vehicles were equipped with pneumatic tyres they became adaptable for all sorts of specialised purposes such as timber extraction, oilfield exploration, and military roles. World War II gave a massive boost to this technology as well as to material (and therefore weight) saving and general production economies.

Left A diesel-engined Mercedes-Benz 8-tonner in British livery, about 1928. The first diesel road-trucks had been built by MAN and Benz four years before. 'Crude-oil' fuel cost 2p a gallon in Britain in the 1920s.

Below A preserved Leyland Beaver TSC9 tanker of 1935. One of the best British 'heavies' of its day, it was powered by Leyland's own six-cylinder, 48 bhp diesel, could carry 7 tons, and had a legal top speed of 32 km/h (20 mph).

The post-war period

The thousands of military vehicles left behind in the far corners of the world after the war were used to start haulage operations, and directly or indirectly led to local manufacture or modification of vehicles using war-surplus vehicle components (just as, in 1919, the French firm Willème had begun by reconditioning American army trucks). Several countries outside Europe and North America had triggered the start of their own industries by the simple expedient of levying prohibitive duties on imported trucks. This also had the effect of encouraging companies such as Ford and General Motors to establish assembly plants in worthwhile markets. Alternatively, local engineering firms acquired licences to build European or American vehicles.

After 1945 local assembly and licenced construction, both using an increasing proportion of locally made components, became mandatory in many countries. The process has continued to the point where today few even partly industrialised countries do not have a motor industry of some sort with tariff barriers to protect it.

The world's major truck manufacturers could see the writing on the wall as fewer and fewer overseas markets were left open to them: they began to unite in order to be large enough to compete at international level.

For all this frenzied financial activity, technical progress in the last three decades has been more in the line of gradual evolution than of the dramatic developments of the late 1920s. As we shall see in Chapter 4, the principal change to power units has been the adoption of forced-air induction by turbochargers, which was first offered in production general-haulage trucks by Volvo in 1954. As exhaust emission control has become closely monitored this has been an ideal way of ensuring complete combustion and 'clean' exhausts. It has had the additional advantage of raising power output per litre and making the most efficient use of increasingly expensive fuel.

To reduce downtime (that is, the period taken up by repairs and maintenance), forward-control trucks were given tilt cabs to improve engine accessibility. The idea had been used occasionally since World War I but Ford (US) was the first major maker to adopt it in 1957 and it spread to Foden in 1962 and then to the whole European industry (BMC was the first British mass-producer to adopt the idea in 1964).

North American truck drivers (especially owner-drivers) still prefer normal control (conventional) trucks, with engine mounted forward of the cab, for the heaviest highway work. In Europe, however, restrictions on overall length of trucks have made forward control or COE (cab-over-engine) the commoner layout; and equivalent restriction are causing a gradual switch to the COE configuration in North America.

One of the most significant European developments of the 1970s was the entry of makers of mass-produced light- and medium-weight trucks — Ford, Bedford, and Peugeot-Citröen Dodge, in particular — into the heaviest categories.

Modern heavy trucks have to be operated intensively to recoup their enormously high initial and operating costs, and there is no place for a vehicle that spends more than the bare minimum in downtime. At the same time they have to be acceptable to the community. For this reason most efforts over the past 10 years have been put into increasing their safety and reliability and decreasing their noise. Productivity has been improved by massive power increases and improved ways of loading and unloading.

Below A 1964 International DCO artic 18-wheeler. When photographed here — at St Paul (Minn.) in July 1978 — it had done more than 3.3 m km (2 m miles). Many highway trucks log over 1.6 m km (1 million miles).

Right Few specialised builders produce more than 2,000 heavy trucks per year, so most (as here at Foden's Sandbach factory) are assembled by hand. Sharing of parts between different models helps to keep prices down.

TRUCK TYPES

The latest trucks designed for long-distance, maximum-weight haulage are all so similar in general appearance that the layman might be forgiven for thinking that they all come from the same builder. The similarity is not surprising when one considers that all the trucks made for a particular weight category in a given country are limited to the same specific overall dimensions. Within these dimensions the designers have to provide the maximum load space while allowing sufficient space for the cab and engine.

The cab

The similarity is carried a stage further by the fact that there are quite a number of specialist cab designers whose cabs are used on models made by different companies. In Britain both Dennis and SD (Shelvoke & Drewry) have used similar Ogle-styled cabs, while until recently Motor Panels, Britain's largest cab maker, was supplying virtually identical cabs for various models made by Guy, SD, Foden, and the Dutch firm FTF. The forward-control cab on Berliet's largest road truck is used by Ford on their Amsterdam-built Transcontinental, while the Club of Four (Volvo, Magirus Deutz, DAF, and SAVIEM) have used almost identical cabs on some of their models; indeed, the Club was formed for the very purpose of sharing production costs of key components among it members. In North America several fire-applicance chassis look the same because they all use Cincinnati steel cabs. The general-haulage trucks made by Dennison in Eire use the same cab as the Finnish Sisu. The Polish Jelcz has a Mercedes-Benz cab on some models, while several IVECO (Industrial Vehicle Corporation) models from three countries have the same basic structure. MAN and SAVIEM have long had technical links, which explains the similarity of their trucks and why these in turn look like the Raba from Hungary and the Roman from Romania, both of which are built under licence from MAN; the MAN subsidiary in Austria, ÖAF (Österreichische Automobilfabrik), also uses the same cab.

Cabs on the big trucks are either day cabs, or sleepers (night cabs) providing a bunk behind the seats. More and more of the latter will be seen as regulations in the European Economic Community (EEC) and elsewhere lessen the number of consecutive hours that a driver is permitted to be behind the wheel. In forward-control cabs the sleeping area is built into the back of the standard structure; on American conventional (normal-control) trucks the sleeper is often a separate 'pod' behind the cab. Future development seems likely to put the sleeping compartment on top of the cab which, on a unit with a high van body behind it, is at present wasted space.

Cab materials

Cab construction varies from country to country and from manufacturer to manufacturer. North America is more weight-conscious, particularly in the western states, than Europe and is prepared to spend what would seem to European eyes to be a disproportionate amount in order to lower a model's dead weight by only a few pounds. The United States is the only country to have all-aluminium cabs in regular production; even the non-specialist heavy-truck makers such as GMC offer aluminium cabs at the top of their ranges, and GMC's Bison conventional also has a glass-fibre bonnet ('hood' in American parlance) and doors. A plastic material, SMC (sheet-moulding compound), which is similar in appearance to glass-fibre, is widely used for bonnets and bumpers in North America, whereas in Britain it is used for complete cab structures to give the same weight-saving and corrosion-resistance advantages as aluminium. Unfortunately, it does not have the same crash resistance as aluminium, although it helps to absorb impact and can take far stronger blows that aluminium before it suffers distortion. SMC has

Preceding two pages For the past 20 years most British ultra-heavy haulage (200 tons and over) has been handled by the Scammell Contractor 6 x 4. Its 395 bhp Cummins engine is harnessed to an 8-speed semi-automatic gearbox.

Right Progressive reduction in the number of consecutive hours a trucker may drive has made sleeper cabs a necessity, and they are now well planned and fitted out. These full-length bunks are in the Ford (Europe) Transcontinental.

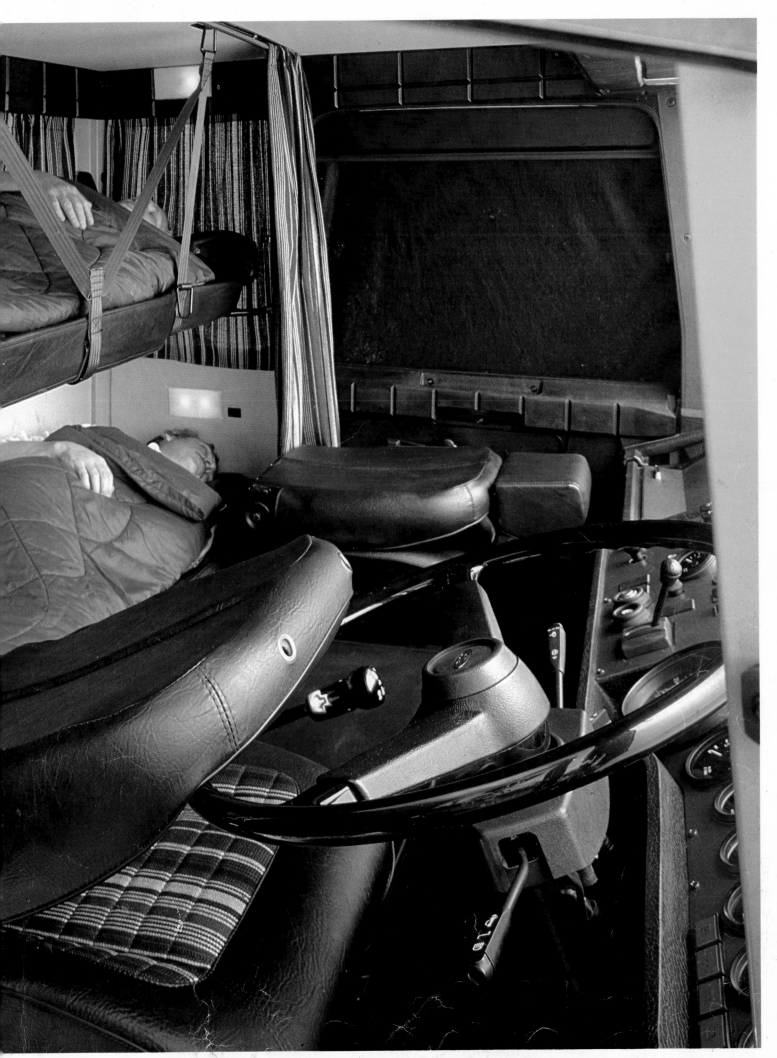

Right Pride of Renault's long-haul rigs, the 1981 cab of the TR305 bristles with driver comforts; two bunks, a sink and cooker between the seats, a fridge, and a TV set in the roof. The cab is basically that of the top-weight Berliet TR305 but with a higher, streamlined roof.

Below Interiors of typical North American and European forward-control cabs. The upper picture is of the White Road Commander all-aluminium cab with its 'saddle vinyl' trim. Note how the inboard half of the dash is angled toward the driver — a design feature of most American forward-control cabs. The cab of the Leyland Constructor 30.21 (lower picture), used mainly for site work, is less fancy but is highly functional and easily cleaned.

enabled the smaller truck manufacturers to have their own individual cab designs because production in this material does not entail the enormous tooling costs involved in working with steel or aluminium.

Sweden has for long had stringent cab-safety regulations, and when its trucks (Volvo and Scania) became more widely seen on European roads from the late 1950s, other manufacturers decided that their own cabs must equal the strength and safety of those of their Swedish rivals. Standard safety tests now include swinging massive weights at the A-posts (the front cab pillars) and simulating roll-overs. SMC cabs will stand up to such tests if they are built around steel safety cages, as on the ERF B-series.

We have already seen how several manufacturers used standardised steel structures from Motor Panels, while Leyland's once-advanced Ergomatic design was made for them by Sankey, one of the GKN companies. The new generation of standard cabs from Motor Panels allow scope for individual frontal-styling treatment that is often applied by their smaller vehicle-making customers. The ERF cab frame is made by Motor Panels, who also engineered, tooled, and now assemble the Seddon Atkinson across-the-range cab, which is trimmed by Seddon Atkinson on delivery.

Foden uses a standard Motor Panels cab for many of the heaviest duty vehicles that require a steel cab, but has developed its own identically styled version which uses GRP (glass-reinforced plastic) panels on a steel frame with aluminium doors. The Leyland T45 Roadtrain has a steel cab made by Motor Panels and probably will be offered with aluminium in place of steel panels in time.

Britain has a lot of truck makers for its size, so inevitably the output from individual factories is small by North American or mainland European standards — under 5,000 chassis per year each from major heavy-truck makers such as Seddon Atkinson, Foden, and ERF. Mainland European makers, which do not have such a highly developed components industry to rely on, tend to make their own cabs and then share them amongst firms with which they have trading or licensing agreements. This greatly increases output of each individual design; this means not only that steel designs are almost invariably used, but that styling changes can be made relatively often. It also means that most Continental trucks have to give away payload to their lighter-weight British and American rivals.

Virtually all forward-control (cab-over-engine) cabs can now be tilted forward through 60 degrees or more to allow easier access to the engine, transmission, and so on. One of the few exceptions is the now-venerable but still widely used Bedford TK, in which the engine is reached via flaps in the rear corners of the cab. (However, the TL, which joined the range in 1980 and will ultimately replace the TK, has a conventional tilt cab.)

Cabs are tilted either by gravity, with muscle and spring assistance, or by hand-worked hydraulic pumps. Most routine maintenance is done through trap doors in the cab floor or opening front panels, so cabs are seldom seen tilted outside the maintenance bay unless a truck breaks down. This is just as well in the case of the more luxurious sleeper cabs, which nowadays are weighed down with every conceivable option, including a kitchen sink. In conventional (normal-control) cabs, access to the engine is provided by a forward-tilting or side-opening ('butterfly') bonnet and/or wings.

One final point on cab design concerns the fore-and-aft measurement of forward-control (cab-over-engine) designs. This measurement is known in American parlance as the BBC (bumper-to-back-of-cab) dimension. In day cabs the BBC of American designs has shrunk considerably over recent years in order to permit the greatest possible load-carrying length within an overall regulation length of 65 ft (19.8 m). BBCs as little as 1.27 m (52 in) are now quite common on day cabs, allowing a tractor to haul an 8.5 m (28 ft) double — that is, an artic semi-trailer and a drawbar trailer, each 8.5 m long — and still leaving room for the semi-trailer to pivot through 90 degrees.

Truck weights and lengths

In Europe the maximum weight permitted for road-going trucks varies from country to country. The extremes are 32.5 tonnes in Britain and Ireland and 50 tonnes in Holland. Italy and Denmark allow 44 tonnes and most of the rest of Europe 38 tonnes. In North America the regulations vary from state to state; some states allow a maximum of 62.5 tonnes but require such trucks to be fitted with a large number of axles to reduce individual tyre loadings. In Europe weight limits vary between 10 and 13 tonnes on single axles and 16 and 21 tonnes on doubles (that is, two closely coupled axles).

Although Britain and Ireland have the lowest overall weight limit, they fall into line on axle weights and so could easily harmonise with their European partners simply by allowing an extra axle on tractors or trailers. This would not require an increase in overall dimensions other than 0.5 m (19½ in) on the overall length of an artic to come into line with the Continental standard of 15.5 m (50.8 ft). As rigid trucks towing drawbar trailers in Britain are already allowed to be 18 m (59 ft) long, this would plainly present few problems.

Axle arrangements

This is a convenient point to deal with truck wheel and axle arrangements. On tractors or rigid trucks these are expressed by a figure such as 4 x 2; this particular figure denotes that the tractor has

European heavy truck and trailer rigs.

Left The rigid truck and drawbar trailer combination is almost as popular as the artic in mainland Europe but is less common in Britain. The truck is a MAN 19:240 powered by a six cylinder, 240 bhp diesel. The gtw is 38 tonnes, divided equally between rigid and trailer.

Below left A typical top-weight articulated truck, consisting of a 4 x 2 tractor and a semi-trailer, and with a maximum gtw of 48 tons. The tractor is the Scania LB141, powered by a 14.2-litre V8 diesel developing 370 bhp and with a synchromesh range-change gearbox giving a total of 10 forward speeds.

four wheels (in fact two axles, because for this purpose double wheels count as one, not two), of which two are driven wheels; likewise 6 x 4 denotes a six-wheeler, of which four wheels are driven. In Europe the top-weight articulated trucks are almost invariably hauled by 4 x 2 tractors (with two or three axles on the semi-trailer), whereas 6 x 4 tractors are commonplace in North America. European rigid trucks towing drawbar trailers at the maximum weight are also usually 4 x 2, as compared to the American 6 x 2 or 6 x 4. In America, rigids for solo use commonly have two or three axles, with an additional 'tag' axle fitted at the back if axle loadings are critical.

In Europe, trucks with four axles invariably have two at the front (with all four wheels steerable) and two at the back; in Britain they are known as eight-leggers, and they are common in Austria, Switzerland, Italy, Spain, Britain, and Holland — and also in Australia. Other countries make eight-wheelers, though usually for use outside their borders. Volvo's eight-wheelers are mostly earmarked for Britain, and so are made at the company's Scotland plant.

Sweden has some very complex laws relating to vehicle operation, and Swedish operators, like their Finnish neighbours, have to pay kilometre tax. This is paid at the rate of roughly 2.5p per kilometre for a typical 20-tonne truck whether it is laden or unladen. There is an additional tax for trailers, so there are advantages in the cassette system, which involves carrying the trailer on the truck when both are unladen. Most Swedish tandem-axle vehicles (that is, vehicles with two close-coupled axles) have a weight transfer device which permits the hindmost axle to be raised clear of the road to turn a six-wheeler into a four-wheeler for unladen running.

Deciding what type of layout to use for which haulage purpose depends on many factors and leads to different answers in different parts of the world. The advantage of the artic (that is, a tractor with semi-trailer) over a rigid has always been that a laden trailer can be dropped (disconnected) and a full or empty trailer coupled in its place in moments. This allows maximum tractor flexibility and productivity.

Modern methods of palletising loads in interchanging standardised containers, however, now allow rigids to achieve turnarounds just as quickly as an artic. The latter is arguably more manoeuvrable than a long rigid; but it is also less stable and liable to 'jack-knife' when braking in slippery conditions. It can also get stuck more easily on poor surfaces when either heavily laden or unladen, especially if it has only one driven axle. In Britain a rigid plus drawbar trailer is limited to the same 32.5 tonne limit as an artic and has most of the same advantages, although it is less manoeuvrable in view of the longer wheelbase of the truck portion.

The only rigid that matches the payload of the rigid-plus-drawbar-trailer or the artic is the eight-legger which, although limited to 30 tonnes, is lighter than most tractor/trailer combinations and so can legally carry a similar payload of around 21 tonnes. It is most widely used where site work is involved and for dense loads such as sand and ballast, although a few are also to be seen in general haulage.

Trailers

Although they may look simple pieces of engineering compared with the vehicles that draw them, trailers are in fact highly sophisticated. This helps to explain why their design and manufacture rests in the hands of the specialists. One of the few exceptions to this rule in recent years has been Scammell, which ultimately found that its truck and trailer sides were not compatible and sold the latter to the Canadian company, York. The worldwide trailer industry is dominated by the American Fruehauf Corporation, which also owns firms in several European countries. British firms include King Truck Equipment, M & G Trailers, and Tasker. Among important European trailer companies are Coder (France), Nuova OMT (Italy), Mol and Van Hool (Belgium), and Kässbohrer (West Germany).

The key to trailer design is, of course, providing a combination of maximum strength and durability with the minimum weight and the best ride characteristics (this last being crucial if a trailer is to carry fragile loads). Some recent designs have had aluminium frames, but in general steel is used with either steel leaf springs or else rubber or air/rubber suspension. Axles usually come from specialist producers, such as Rockwell, and tyre equipment varies between 'super singles' or conventional twins; three-axle trailers usually have singles to minimise tyre scrub when cornering. Usually the only surplus weight carried is the landing gear for when an artic semi-trailer has to stand away from its tractor. (The tractor, of course, also carries some dead-weight in the shape of its 'fifth wheel', the name given to the circular platform where the semi-trailer is attached.)

Trailers (and many rigids, for that matter) mostly have platform or van bodywork. Some are so-called 'skeletals', which have no bodywork, just twist-locks for retaining the lugs on the standardised containers widely used on railways and in worldwide shipping. These twist-locks are sometimes also built into platform bodies.

Refrigerated bodies (or 'reefers', as they are called in North America and Britain) have heavily insulated walls and carry a refrigeration plant outside on the front powered by a small independent diesel engine, which runs continuously whenever the trailer carries a load. Among the best known of these units are those made by Petter of Britain and Thermo King of the United States.

Tankers for carrying liquid in bulk come in various shapes and sizes, and there is a growing preference for elliptical- rather than circular-section designs because they make for a lower centre of gravity. This is taken a stage further on some tanker semi-trailers, where the tank tapers longitudinally, with a fatter, underslung middle. This is particularly popular on bulk powder tankers, which carry their own separate engine-driven pumps for sucking or blowing loads. Some tanks are insulated to maintain viscous loads such as tar or chocolate in the liquid state.

A relatively recent trailer development has been 'curtain siders' which, as their name implies, are bodies with fixed ends and tops which can be loaded from the sides by forklift truck and then turned into vans by drawing heavy-duty side curtains, which are strong enough to retain the load if it should slip. These bodies have the advantage of light weight and resistance to damage — something to which aluminium-sided vans are particularly prone.

Self-loaders

A familiar sight on rigid-platform trucks is a small hydraulic crane behind the cab to enable them to be loaded by the driver. These have done away with the need for drivers' mates and help to save expensive down-time. Tippers on either rigid chassis or semi-trailers usually have a subframe attached to the body to give adequate strength when raised hydraulically. Some tipping trailers carry their own engine-driven hydraulic pumps so that they can be used even with tractors not equipped with pumps.

Maximum-capacity six- and eight-wheel rigids are preferred for brick transport because of the minimal space needed for their dense loads and because they can have double-drive axles to avoid bogging when delivering to building sites. These trucks often have their own hydraulic crane mounted at the approximate mid-point of the load (or else able to traverse its length) so that outstretch does not have to be too great.

A variation on the self-loading theme is the skip loader, which carries its own pivoting gantry and outriggers and can swing laden skips on board from the rear. Even skips are now becoming highly sophisticated; some regularly used at certain sites (as, for example, at shopping precincts) are equipped to be attached to mobile compression plants so that they can be stuffed with a worthwhile load. Most skip loaders carry one skip at a time, but some rigid sixes have space for two (or three with a drawbar trailer).

Another idea for self-loading which has been gaining in popularity in recent years is the demountable body, which either has jack-up legs to enable it to be loaded or unloaded from its carrier, or else is

separated when the chassis of the vehicle under it is lowered hydraulically or mechanically. In this way an individual rigid truck can be used with a wide variety of body types; it gains the flexibility of the tractor and detachable semi-trailers and can be used to carry pre-loaded bodies at all times and avoid wasteful unladen running. A variation on this theme is the hydraulically lowered body. In a typical example, the Brimec system, an apparently conventional platform body can be slid back and tipped so that the goods can be winched or driven onto it from the rear. The Multi-Lift system is similar and can be used with various body types. On a smaller scale is the tail lift, which in the travelling position acts as the vehicle's tailgate but which when tilted horizontally can be used for raising and lowering loads. This type is widely used by the distributive trades and especially by domestic-appliance manufacturers.

Just as these modern methods of loading and unloading speed turnround, so do the latest load-restraint systems. The days when a driver spent half an hour or more securing his load with lengths of rope and lots of clever knots and hitches are virtually gone. Now all

Above A top-weight Peterbilt 6 x 4 with reefer (refrigerated) semi-trailer. This is what the Americans call an 18-wheeler, although strictly speaking it is a six-wheel tractor with a four-wheel semi because double tyres count as one when classifying truck-wheel arrangements. The Thermo King refrigeration plant on the front of the semi works on the same general principles as a domestic fridge.

Right Fuso is Mitsubishi's heavy-truck marque. This 230 bhp rigid has an unusual self-loading system in which the rear of the body is tilted to ground level when the front end is raised on hydraulically powered struts behind the cab. The load is driven or winched aboard.

sorts of ratchet systems and over-centre buckles (as used on car seat belts) take the place of knots, and rope has given way to nylon webbing, with chain for portions of the load that chafe. Tarpaulins are still used, although curtain siders or dropside bodies — with their own trackway on the side down which the sheet unrolls like a window blind — are taking over fast. For loads that can be exposed to the weather, such as bricks, nets are the simplest and safest answer and help to give the driver and operator peace of mind. The driver is responsible for his load and can be in serious legal trouble if bits of it drop off into the road.

Completely custom-built trucks, in which the chassis as well as the body are made for a specific purpose, are considered in the next chapter, but the list of body 'specials' is almost limitless: transit concrete mixers, car transporters, refuse compactors, gully emptiers, wreckers, pigeon carriers, livestock transporters, standby generators, tar sprayers, and mobile libraries are just a few.

As trucks become adapted to more and more purposes, it is not surprising to find road transport growing at the expense of rail, canal, and coastal shipping. The only means of transport to have shown any growth apart from road transport in Britain in recent years have been freight aircraft and pipelines — and both of these are of small importance when compared with the more than 82 per cent of all goods which go by road. Major efforts have been made to shift traffic to the railways, but the latter's lack of flexibility and coverage — especially since the post-war line closures — and the fact that goods still have to be delivered to and from stations or container terminals by road, has always frustrated this. As it is, even if British Rail carried 50 per cent more goods than it does at present, this would decrease road tonnage by only about 6 per cent — and in terms of vehicle numbers this could easily be made good by increasing the truck weight limit from 32.5 to 38 tonnes.

At present some 60 per cent of Britain's international trade is handled by container. The farcical situation exists that, when loaded to internationally acceptable standards, the largest containers are too heavy to be legally transported by truck in Britain. Every day continental trucks arrive at British ports with scientifically packed loads that have to be split between two vehicles in order to conform to the law. This greatly increases transport costs, causes unnecessary delays, and means that standardised 40 ft (12.19 m) containers have to be loaded below capacity, thus wasting valuable ship-cargo space. In spite of all these artificial constraints, and the fact that a heavy truck in Britain pays something like £1,500 a year in road tax and perhaps £3,000 a year in fuel tax, there still appears to be no viable alternative to road transport.

SPECIALISED CHASSIS

Above The largest specialist fire-appliance builder in the United States is American LaFrance, which makes both chassis and fire-fighting equipment. This Century-series model has Cummins or Detroit Diesel engines of up to 380 bhp; automatic transmission is optional.

Above right An Italian Perlini 605D crash tender with Baribbi equipment. Fully laden, its 31.5 tonnes will accelerate from zero to 80 km/h (50 mph) in 45 sec by means of twin rear-mounted Detroit Diesels totalling 530 hp and an Allison (GM) automatic gearbox.

Right The Oshkosh M-23 is one of the largest crash tenders in production, with all four axles driven. It is powered by front- and rear-mounted Detroit V8s totalling 984 bhp. Its water tank holds 23,000 l (6,077 gal) and its foam tank 1,950 l (517 gal), and it can discharge water and foam simultaneously at the rate of 3,407 l/min (750 gal/min) each.

Preceding two pages The German firm Faun builds carriers for permanently fitted mobile cranes with lifting capacities of 25 to 500 tons. This particular giant is powered by a Cummins 350 bhp diesel and is steered on all 12 wheels. Two of the four outriggers used to stabilise the vehicle when the crane is operating can be seen in retracted position between the innermost two axles.

All heavy trucks nowadays are to some extent specialised: most models are available with, for instance, a long list of engine and transmission options to make them ideally suited to such differing requirements as sustaining 95 km/h (59 mph) or more on the highway — many of the American heavies are geared to exceed 145 km/h (90 mph), in spite of the 88.5 km/h (55 mph) limit — or lugging gravel up a 1 in 5 hill from an off-road pit. However, if a truck is required for a highly specific purpose it is often uneconomic to modify a model in series production, and then the project is usually taken over by one of the custom builders.

In the advanced industrial countries there are more of these firms than there are major producers. Most of them are relatively small and geared to hand-assembly: each truck may take weeks to build, and this of course limits production and raises costs.

Fire engines and crash tenders

As well as the firms prepared to turn their expertise to many different types of custom truck there are the ones that concentrate most of their efforts on trucks for one or two particular purposes. A prime example is the fire-appliance chassis. There are several dozen builders, and only a few of them make more than 100 appliances each year. In North America individual brigades are often under local control with perhaps one man or a small committee buying an extremely personalised fire appliance only once every 20 years or so. The buyer has the option of buying a commercial pumper or escape (as specialist fire-fighting equipment on a general-haulage chassis is called), or a custom vehicle. Some of these are built by fire-equipment specialists such as Crown Firecoach or FMC on special chassis from custom-truck builders such as Spartan, Hendrickson, Duplex, Oshkosh, and others. With others the entire vehicle is assembled in one factory, as in the case of American LaFrance, Ward LaFrance, Hahn, Maxim, Seagrave (a subsidiary of FWD), Peter Pirsch, Pierce, and several others. All these appliances are built to an extremely high specification and differ from conventional truck chassis in being lower, more powerful (350 bhp in a vehicle of around 12 tonnes total weight is common), and often equipped with automatic transmission. Although most of them are now diesel powered, many have until recently used V-12 petrol engines.

In Europe the best known fire-appliance makers are Dennis of Britain and Magirus of West Germany, although SD has recently joined the field; Mercedes-Benz and Dodge have fire-chassis departments, just as Mack does in North America.

Another and even more specialised type of fire appliance is the crash tender for use at airports. This is designed to get to the scene of an aircraft fire in the shortest possible time over runways or rough ground and to carry enough foam compound to be able to smother even a jumbo jet in seconds. The first in the civil aviation field in Europe in the 1950s was the Thornycroft (now Scammell) Nubian, although the idea had been conceived during World War II, when the U.S. Air Force used converted military trucks. Today the chief crash-tender builders are Oshkosh, Walter, and several of the makers of complete fire appliances in North America, RFW in Australia, Faun and Kaelble in West Germany, Perlini in Italy, and Reynolds-Boughton, SD, and Unipower in Britain. The British models are based on all-wheel-drive chassis (either 4 x 4 or 6 x 6) which are sent to fire-fighting specialists such as Chubb and Carmichael to be equipped with bodywork, pumps, and other equipment.

By way of an example of capabilities, the largest 8 x 8 Oshkosh can reach its top speed of 80 km/h (50 mph) in 55 seconds at a laden weight of 59,358 kg (58.3 tons), which includes about 25,000 litres (6,600 gal) of water and foam compounds. It can climb 60 per cent gradients, run on a 26-degree side slope, and negotiate 457 mm (18 inch) walls. Power is provided by two V-8 Detroit diesels each developing 492 bhp. Many of the largest crash tenders are rear or mid-engined with central driving positions at the front. All have foam monitors above the front and usually a barrage of sprays pointing forward to keep burning fuel away from the vehicle.

Off-road dumpers

If crash tenders are the giants in terms of power and speed, the prize for size and power must go to the dump trucks. From modest beginnings in the 1930s, when quarry owners and contractors decided that strengthened tippers were not strong enough to stand up to a life lived permanently off the road, special vehicles have been developed which in many cases do not comply with the regulations that apply to ordinary road vehicles. With no constraints governing the size of vehicles in open-cast mining projects around the world, dump trucks grew dramatically through the 1950s and today the largest can carry several hundred tons at a time. Some of the best-known names in giant dump trucks are American, notably Caterpillar, Cline, Dart, Euclid (now owned by Mercedes-Benz), Lectra Haul (Unit Rig), Rimpull, Terex (now owned by IBH of West Germany), V-Con, and WABCO. The best-known Europeans are the German Faun and Kaelble, the British Aveling-Barford and Heathfield, the Italian Astra and Perlini, and the Russian BELAZ. The chief Japanese marque is the Komatsu. The design and construction of the largest dumpers is quite different from that of highway vehicles. Some replace rear suspension with large rubber blocks. Front suspension is seldom by conventional steel springs but rather by rubber or else by means of columns filled with compressed oil and nitrogen or some other non-freezing substance.

Vast locomotive diesel engines with 12 or even 16 cylinders produce 700 to 1600 bhp in typical installations and deliver their drive to the rear wheels via double-, triple-, or even quadruple-reduction axles (the final reduction is often by a gear train in the wheel hubs). Dump trucks of more than 100 tons capacity usually have diesel-electric transmission, as in the case of the aptly named Lectra Haul from Unit Rig (the largest of which is a two-axle truck for 200-ton loads), in which the engine drives a generator which powers electric wheel motors. Some, like the Dart dumpers, stick to conventional Allison automatic transmissions above 100 tons, and gearshifts on most of the smaller trucks are also automatic or semi-automatic to avoid risking appalling damage that a driver could cause with so much weight and power to control. One of the largest dumpers

Above WABCO 3200B Haulpak 6 x 4 is a typical American ultra-large off-road dumper. Its 2,475 bhp Detroit Diesel locomotive engine drives a generator that provides traction to the four rear wheels. Capacity is 235 tons.

Below White Western Star 4900 dumper, for both highway and off-road operations, is powered by a 380 bhp Caterpillar 3406 turbocharged diesel.

of all, the 3,000 bhp 8 x 6 V-Con Model 3006, is so vast — it is no less than 8.5 m (28 ft) wide — that it has to be assembled on site.

Dump trucks are one of the few classes of heavy vehicles to use disc brakes — usually in the transmission or on the back axle, with drum brakes at the front. The mechanical-drive trucks often have engine retarders and the electric-drive trucks invariably have a control for switching the drive motors into generators for dynamic braking. Bodies are massively strong and are often designed so that exhaust gases are ducted along the box sections to warm the body and aid discharge of sticky loads, especially in frosty weather. Most of the largest dump trucks have rear-dump bodies, although some are used to haul bottom-dump trailers instead, often in open-cast coal pits.

Lower down the weight range are dump trucks for 20- or 30-ton loads; these are more closely related to normal trucks, except that they are built with no unladen-weight constraints. Foden and Haulamatic are both well known in this category, as are the flexible-frame truck makers like Volvo-BM, Werklust (from Holland), Moxy (from Norway), and DJB (Britain). On these a two-wheel portion that steers by pivoting, and carries the driver and engine, is permanently attached to a one- or two-axle dump trailer; the drive layout is usually 4 x 4 or 6 x 4. Similar vehicles are also used for timber extraction with so-called pole trailers and their own self-loading cranes.

Refuse collection

Closer still to normal highway trucks are those vehicles built specially for refuse collection. Series-production chassis are sometimes used, but in general chassis as well as compaction bodies are made by specialists. This is because very robust frames and transmissions are needed to allow a vehicle to be suitable for both stop-start collection work and also relatively high-speed transit to increasingly distant dumping grounds. Driving conditions are often rough at the dumps, and frame distortion could easily lead to expensive damage to sophisticated bodywork when tipping on uneven ground.

In Britain Dennis, SD, and Seddon Atkinson make most of the purpose-built refuse-collection chassis; the first two also make much of their own bodywork, as does their German counterpart, Faun. All have crew cabs able to house the driver and loading gang. In North America most of the special garbage chassis are for a slightly different purpose, that of lifting skips from the front and depositing their contents in special compression bodies. The resulting machine is typically a forward-control 6 x 2 or 6 x 4 with very-low-mounted cab to allow the pick-up arms to work through the smallest possible arc. Mack, CCC (Crane Carrier Company), and Master Truck are among several American firms making such chassis, which normally have their cabs set well forward of the front axle and their engines between body and cab.

Local delivery

Another breed of special vehicle has been adopted for the brewery and soft-drinks trade. Such vehicles need to make many small, local deliveries, but have to carry heavy loads. In Holland DAF makes a special brewery vehicle with a central backbone chassis, which allows the two sections of 'bed' on either side of it to be much nearer the ground than the bed above a normal parallel-girder chassis. The same objective is achieved in Britain by Bedford and Ford, who fit very small wheels and tyres, and a second steering axle well behind the first so that the net load is unaffected by what would otherwise be inadequate tyres. Primrose does similar conversions to Leyland and other chassis, and has also made a rigid eight-wheeler to the same concept out of a two-axle Leyland. SD makes a brewery truck with a drop-frame as on a bus.

Mobile cranes

An even more specialised variety of truck is the type — made by Faun, Titan, Mol CCC, CVS, Mitsubishi, Consolidated Dynamics, and others — used as the permanent base for mobile cranes. Sometimes the crane manufacturer itself makes the chassis, but often this work is left to the specialists, and some remarkable designs have resulted for cranes of from 50 to as much as 1,000 tonnes capacity. Obviously the bigger the lifting capacity of the crane the bigger must be its size. On the other hand there is little point in making it self-propelled unless it can be driven safely and legally on public roads. The largest models have rigid axles with five, six, or even seven axles — all but the centre one or two axles steered. Drive goes to all or most axles to permit site

Left Refuse-collection chassis are made either by specialists or, as with this 1976 Saurer 5DF, are converted from heavy-duty tipper models. The 5DF is powered by Saurer's 250 bhp six-cylinder unit.

Above Haulage of the largest and heaviest loads often requires both a tow and a pusher tractor. Here a nuclear reactor shell is pulled by an Autocar 6 x 4 and pushed by a converted Autocar eight-legger.

use and the cab is very low-slung to avoid interference with the jib. A vital part of the equipment is built-in outriggers that can be extended to provide four steel legs to stabilise the whole machine when in use as a crane. Suspension is normally pretty rudimentary, and often the only flexibility on the rear axles is provided by attaching them to centrally pivoted 'balance beams'.

Dock and harbour trucks

A relatively recent type of truck, produced by Bollnas in Sweden, Mol in Belgium, Douglas and Reliance-Mercury in Britain, Ottawa, Ibex, and Coleman in the US, DAF in Holland, and several others, is the ro-ro (roll-on, roll-off) or yard/dock-spotter tractor. This looks much like the tractive unit from a normal artic outfit, except that it usually has only a half-cab (that is, the cab extends across only half the width of the truck), and duplicated controls to allow the vehicle to be driven forwards or backwards with equal facility. Another difference is that

its fifth wheel (the mounting point for the semi-trailer) can be raised or lowered to suit the widest possible variety of semi-trailers. As its name suggests, this type of tractor is used for manoeuvring semi-trailers at ports and freight yards, and for loading them onto ro-ro ships or ferries. This means that haulage firms' tractors do not have to waste time at the dockside — or take up precious space in ships' holds. Most ro-ro tractors have automatic transmission and extremely robust construction to stand up to their 'bumper-car' existence and can haul semi-trailer loads of up to 50 tonnes.

Extra-heavy road haulage

So far as highway vehicles are concerned, the most spectacular special-purpose trucks are the tractors for extra-heavy haulage. Gearing is such that it is traction——which depends on the ability of the tyres to grip the road — not power, that is the limiting factor to what can be towed. The tractors are usually ballasted with up to 30 tons of weights over the driven rear wheels to give them adequate traction, and they are capable of towing all that a railway shunting locomotive could handle on similar gradients. On rare occasions, indivisible loads of over 1,000 tons have been handled on short hauls.

The Canadian firm Pacific, owned by International Harvester, builds giant six-wheelers for working either singly or in unit. A 700 bhp

Willème 8 x 8 from France was claimed to be able to pull 300 tons up an 18-degree slope. The ÖAF Jumbo (or MAN Jumbo as it is known outside Austria) has a 16-litre, V-10 MAN 400 bhp diesel and can cope with a gtw (gross train weight) of up to 250 tonnes. A similar vehicle converted from the largest Mercedes-Benz by Titan has a 21-litre, 400 bhp engine and ZF automatic gearbox. Kenworth, Autocar, Oshkosh, and others make massive 'conventional' tractors in North America, while in Britain the Leyland special-vehicle division at Scammell's Watford factory is the chief exponent. The Scammell Contractor 6 x 4 with 395 bhp Cummins engine is frequently expected to handle a gtw of 240 tons and the new S 24 model can operate at 300 tonnes gtw. An even more powerful Scammell is the Commander, with a 625 bhp Rolls-Royce V-12 engine. This can pull loads of 65 tonnes at 61 km/h (38 mph), and far greater weights at lower speeds. Most of these ultra-heavyweight tractors have torque-converter transmissions with either manual or automatic gear changing.

In mainland Europe some of the extra-heavy articulated trucks have semi-trailers with one or two extra axles at the front which are suspended from the semi's coupling to the 'fifth wheel'. This imposition of part of the load on the tractor's driven wheels eliminates the need for ballast. In some cases, too, the trailers are also powered.

Left Many of the largest American concrete carriers discharge to the front, operations being controlled by the driver from within the cab. Typical is the Oshkosh B Series, with rear-mounted engine of up to 290 bhp driving through a manual or automatic gearbox.

Right Highly specialised is the Fabco WT 6 x 6 harvesting truck, capable of moving at very slow speeds between rows of lettuce or other produce and then rushing the load to market. The driver sits in a half-cab on the left side of the chassis, with the Detroit Diesel on the right side. Fabco is a subsidiary of the Fruehauf Corporation, the world's largest builder of highway trailers.

All-wheel-drive trucks

Numerous firms make off-road vehicles for many purposes. These can be relatively conventional trucks whose traction is improved by fitting driven front axles; or highly sophisticated machines such as the Czechoslovakian Tatra with 6 x 6 or 8 x 8 and very flexible independent suspension to keep each wheel in firm contact with the ground over the roughest terrain. Among several American specialists in this field is FWD, which has been making all-wheel-drive vehicles for some 70 years; other firms simply instal 4 x 4 and 6 x 6 drive trains in otherwise conventional model ranges.

West Germany and Switzerland in particular are enthusiastic users of all-wheel-drive, on/off-road tippers, and the principal firms (MAN, Mercedes-Benz, Magirus, and Saurer) build suitable chassis. In Britain Bedford makes one of the few relatively cheap 4 x 4 medium to heavy trucks. Few of these, however, are bought for civilian purposes: as elsewhere, it is the Army that buys most cross-country trucks. An example of extreme specialisation in all-wheel-drive vehicles is furnished by the American firm of Fabco, which makes a 6 x 6 model specifically for harvesting lettuces from California fields. These fields are irrigated and then allowed to partially dry, hence the need for 6 x 6 and the ability to crawl down carefully spaced rows at less than 1.6 km/h (1 mph) while being loaded. Then the truck has to be able to rush to the market, perhaps two hours away, at the legal maximum of 88.6 km/h (55 mph). These two seemingly incompatible needs are catered for by a five-speed gearbox, with a three-speed auxiliary box and a two-speed transfer box, giving 30 forward gears!

Another location where all-wheel-drive is vital is in the desert, where it is usefully allied with semi-smooth, large-section tyres. Here the heaviest trucks are invariably 6 x 6 types by firms such as Kenworth, Oshkosh, Pacific, Mol, Magirus, Scammell, and International. They are usually designed to be able to load themselves by winching enormous unit loads, such as skid-mounted pumps and compressors, over rollers on the rear of their bodies (which do not extend beyond the rear axle). The winches are located under massive cages or shields ('headache racks') behind the cabs, and the generic term 'rough-neck' is applied to this type of truck. Some of the biggest come from Kenworth, and have twin radiators, 700 bhp engines, and a gvw of 72.75 tonnes. MOL and Magirus use Deutz V-12 air-cooled diesels of around 400 bhp to eliminate the boiling and gasket troubles that tend to plague water-cooled units in desert operations.

Specials

The list of custom-built trucks is as varied as it is long. In addition to the ones mentioned so far there are dozens of one-off designs. An example of this is the Douglas truck that was built specially for cleaning the walls and ceiling of the river Mersey road tunnel. It would take a dozen books to describe all the specials and custom-builts, but a few more should be mentioned to indicate the range. A couple of types that are now familiar to air travellers are the low-profile aircraft-refuelling truck, and the scissor-lift truck for loading and unloading aircraft (the various freighters and airliners have cargo doors at widely differing heights). Then there are the American all-wheel-drive specials for delivering building blocks and for mixing concrete. The latter are typically 6 x 6 designs, and are made chiefly by CCC, Oshkosh, Chuting Star, and (in Canada) Flextruck. Many of these very large transit mixers differ from the European variety in that they have rear engines and the mixer drum is angled forwards for front discharge. This gives the seated driver the advantage of being able to see exactly where he is placing the concrete and allows the mixing and discharge controls to be in the small cab. CVS now makes a similar chassis in Italy.

The Flextruck has an articulated frame, a 305 bhp rear-mounted Detroit diesel, and its front three axles are driven while one or two undriven tag axles (the hindmost raisable) are at the back. The Oshkosh B Series has a rigid frame and similar tag or pusher axles. It also has an optional Load Span feature which consists of a hydraulically raisable tag axle well behind the rear engine pod. When lowered for use, the axle greatly increases the wheelbase length and so allows greater payloads in certain states where, without it, the local regulations governing axle loadings and spread would lessen the truck's cost-effectiveness.

Another speciality of Oshkosh and its rivals Walter, Duplex, and Marmon Transmotive, is utility trucks for local highway authorities. These are 4 x 4 trucks used for tipping and general road-mending duties for most of the year but convertible into heavy-duty snowploughs in the winter. The Oshkosh P Series features differentials that will automatically lock if a 'torque proportioner' senses any loss of wheel grip. The Walter has a similar system, and also an unusual drive arrangement in which the weight of the vehicle is carried on normal dead-beam axles but the drive is fed by independent shafts to ring gearing in each wheel hub.

Military trucks form a whole specialised field in themselves, although the high cost of custom-built chassis is nowadays leading to replacement of the weirder designs by standard production types. High-mobility 8 x 8s from Faun and MAN, and 6 x 6 models from Foden and Scania do the really difficult work in Europe, but cheaper 6 x 4 and 8 x 4s are also specified for simple road-borne supply duties. Lancia makes amphibious 4 x 4 trucks, and others are built in the Soviet Union and North America. Some of the Soviet army's all-wheel-drive vehicles have a facility for adjusting tyre pressures on the move, so that the trucks can keep going if conditions change suddenly.

Specialised trucks are nowadays found all over the world, on and off the highway, and in every kind of conditions. They carry supplies over the Arctic tundra, across deserts, and in underground mines. Yet wherever they go, and however unusual their job, specialised trucks are closely related to their regular-production cousins we see every day in town or on the motorways. The basic engineering problems of engine, transmission, brakes, and so on apply to all trucks, so it's time we had a closer look at these subjects.

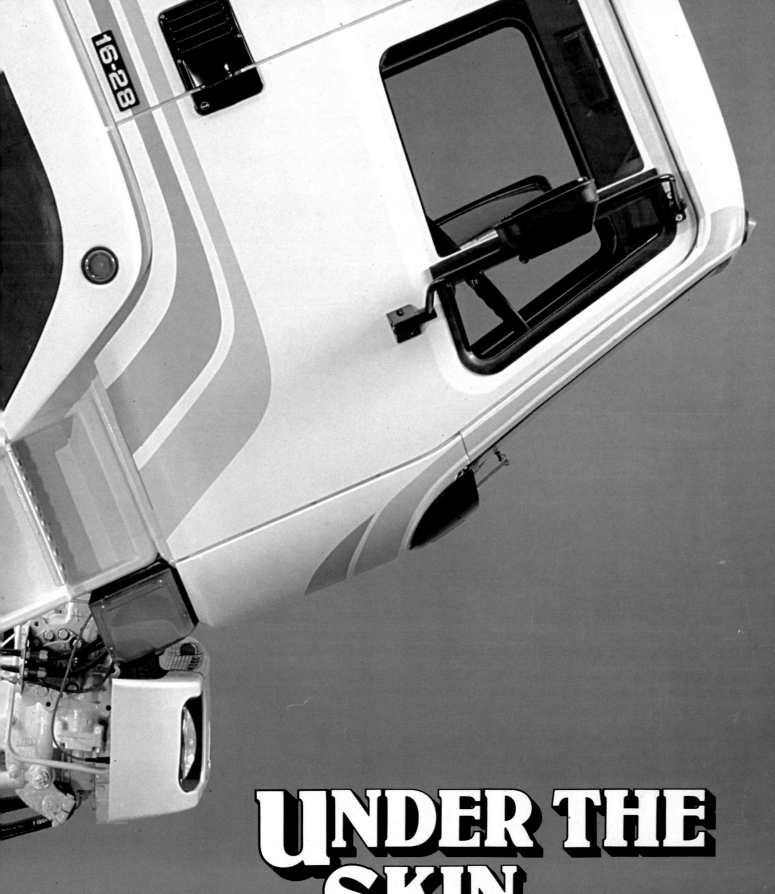

UNDER THE SKIN

Power and quietness, strength and lightness, durability and economy: these are a few of the sometimes conflicting needs of the heavy truck. Some of them are legal requirements: a truck's permitted level of engine noise, and the type or quantity of waste products it is allowed to exhaust into the atmosphere, are controlled to varying degrees in many countries. Not so well known is the fact that a number of industrialised countries insist on a minimum power-to-weight ratio (usually 7 bhp per ton), so that heavy trucks can keep pace with the rest of the traffic on busy urban and trunk roads.

The fleet operator is looking for a truck that is economical in operation and inexpensive to maintain. But these virtues, too, may be incompatible. For the operator of a large fleet of maximum-weight trucks, which may do little better than 7 miles per gallon, a model that offers an improvement of, say, 0.1 mpg may have a decisive advantage: in a 50-truck fleet this could offer a saving of £10,000 or so a year. On the other hand, this saving in thirst may have been achieved by the truck maker at the expense of greater mechanical sophistication — and this would not only have raised the truck's purchase price but would probably also involve more complex, and therefore more expensive, maintenance procedures.

Engines

How the requirements for greater economy, power, and efficiency are met by the heavy-truck engineers is a fascinating topic and one which has many different interpretations around the world. In very general terms, so far as engines are concerned there are two courses open to the designer. One is to opt for relatively small, lightweight engines that rely on speed and sophistication to achieve adequate power outputs. The torque of such engines — that is, the usable power at

the crankshaft — tends to be low, so the gearbox, propeller shaft, and driven axle(s) can also be relatively light. This saves weight and materials (and therefore price, although this advantage is largely negated by the greater precision required in the manufacture of the components). It will also save fuel if the engine is always working hard and at speeds near its maximum efficiency.

The alternative is to use big, lightly stressed engines. Although these need stronger transmissions, their greater torque means that they need fewer gear ratios, and so may save a little weight in that way. An engine of, say, 14 litres capacity does not have to weigh

twice as much as a 7-litre unit: to some extent the difference between them is the difference in volume of the cylinders. The 14-litre unit will need a heavier crankshaft, pistons, and crankcase, but most of the other components could be little different in weight irrespective of the capacity of the engine.

These concepts are so fundamentally different that it might be thought that one or other would show a clear-cut advantage. The fact that they do not is obvious from the number of fleets in Britain made up both of maximum-weight 6.7-litre Volvo F7s and of 14-litre Cummins-engined Seddon Atkinsons or ERFs of broadly similar brake-horsepower.

Sweden and the Netherlands have been keen proponents of 'small' engines while Britain, Italy, West Germany, France, Japan, and the United States favour large ones. As a broad generalisation the rest of the world falls between the two camps and finds about 11 litres adequate for many of its largest trucks or else buys large proprietary engines from elsewhere.

To achieve satisfactory power outputs the smaller engines have to be turbocharged. A turbocharger is a type of compressor driven by an engine's exhaust gases. It forces air under pressure into the combustion chambers, so increasing power by one third or more. A more recent development is after-cooling (or inter-cooling), of which DAF was a pioneer in Europe. The air from the turbocharger, being compressed, is hot. The effect of turbocharging can be considerably enhanced if the air is cooled — and thereby made more dense — as it is forced into the combustion chamber. This is the job of the after-cooler. Turbocharging and after-cooling help an engine to burn fuel more efficiently — and therefore more economically — than a normally aspirated engine, and to emit cleaner exhaust.

The advantages of turbocharging were soon applied also to the traditional, large-capacity engines — with dramatic results. Initially, the extra pressures caused bearing and cylinder-head troubles, but once these were resolved turbocharging led to astonishing increases in efficiency. The typical 14-litre Cummins, developing 250 bhp in normal trim, was found to be quite capable of pushing out a reliable 475 bhp when twin-turbocharged and after-cooled. In many instances all this additional power was unnecessary, but it led indirectly to a new breed of remarkably efficient 'de-speeded' engines. The idea was to make a diesel engine develop its maximum torque both at the lowest possible speed and over the widest possible revolution band. MAN, Mack, Renault, Mercedes-Benz, and Leyland among the truck manufacturers, and Cummins, Caterpillar, and Rolls-Royce among the engine makers have adopted this strategy with great success. The slower an engine runs, the less fuel it will use

and the less frictional wear its moving parts will suffer. The wider the rev. band at which maximum or near maximum torque is available, the simpler the transmission can be and the fewer the gear ratios. Where the driver of a normal engine would have to change down a gear to obtain the greater power available at higher engine revolutions, the 'torque-rise' engine (as the new type is called) just hangs on. In North America, Mack was a pioneer in this field with its Maxidyne engines; in Europe, Renault has been a leader. Mack's 300 Series engine gives between 950 and 1,464 Nm (703 and 1,083 lbf.ft) of torque all the way between 1,100 rpm and its maximum of

2,100 rpm, and it allows the use of a gearbox with only five forward ratios. The Cummins E290 14-litre engine reaches peak torque at a mere 1,300 rpm and remains close to the peak for several hundred revs. By way of comparison the 9.6-litre Volvo diesel's power output is similar (300 as opposed to 290 bhp) but its peak torque over a much smaller rev band is only 1,030 Nm (762 lbf.ft) as compared with the Cummins' 1,261 Nm (933 lbf.ft).

The great majority of big-truck engines nowadays are water-cooled, four-stroke (four-cycle in US parlance) diesels; but several other types are used. In the United States General Motors'

Pages 34-5 Leyland 16.28 Day Cab 40-tonne gcw tractor, one of the T45 Roadtrain series, powered by Leyland's 12.47-litre 280 bhp T12 turbocharged engine.

Far left A popular straight-six diesel, the Cummins 14-litre engine develops from 240 bhp (as in this NT240 model) to 450bhp according to the degree of turbocharging. The turbo unit, partly cut away, is at left.

Near left Mack Maxidyne 300 Series engine. Mack pioneered 'torque-rise' engines with its first Maxidyne unit in 1966. This model develops 285 bhp and delivers a peak torque of 1,464 Nm (1,083 lbf.ft) at 1,200 rpm. The radiator-like component is the after-cooling unit.

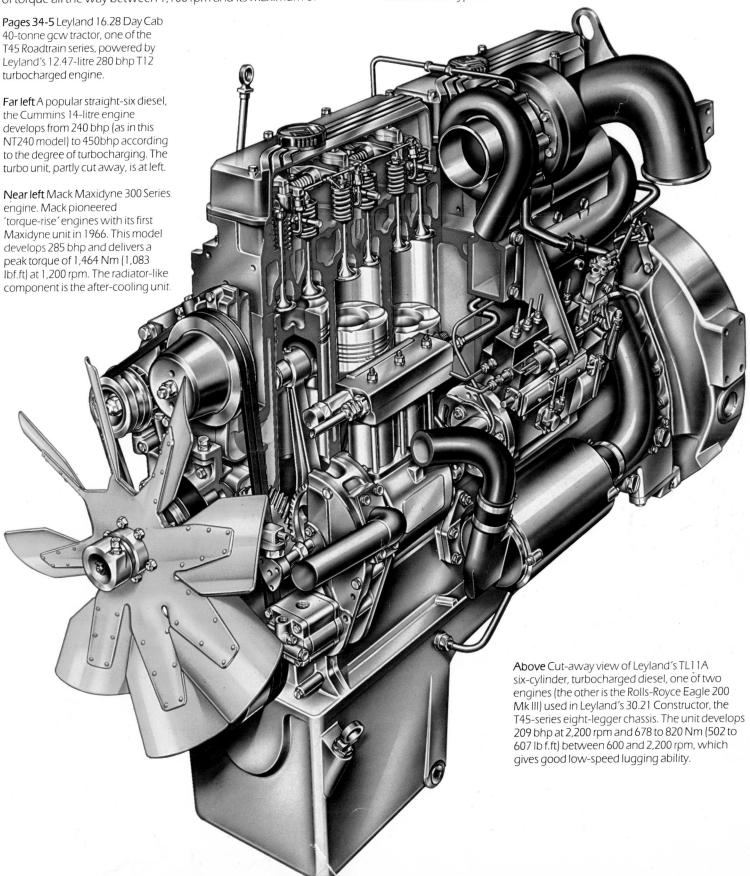

Above Cut-away view of Leyland's TL11A six-cylinder, turbocharged diesel, one of two engines (the other is the Rolls-Royce Eagle 200 Mk III) used in Leyland's 30.21 Constructor, the T45-series eight-legger chassis. The unit develops 209 bhp at 2,200 rpm and 678 to 820 Nm (502 to 607 lb f.ft) between 600 and 2,200 rpm, which gives good low-speed lugging ability.

subsidiary, Detroit Diesel, although it offers some four-strokes, is firmly wedded to the two-stroke principle. At one time Commer, Krupp, MAZ, Foden, and others also built two strokes, but now Detroit is the only major producer; its engines are used in several makes of truck on both sides of the Atlantic. The claimed advantages of the two-stroke are that it is more efficient because every other stroke of the piston in each cylinder is a power stroke compared with every fourth in its rival. It is also simpler, smaller, lighter, and theoretically simpler to service. In recent years Detroit Diesel has made three series of diesel engines in which the volume of each cylinder is respectively 869, 1,164, and 1,508 cc. In spite of the fact that engines in each series are available in both in-line and V configurations, the standardised cylinder dimensions allow many of the engines to have various parts in common and so reduce unit costs.

Another departure from conventional design is the air-cooled diesel. The two main European proponents of air-cooling are Tatra of Czechoslovakia and Deutz of West Germany. Deutz is, interestingly, the firm for which Dr Nikolaus Otto produced the first-ever four-stroke engine in 1872. Today, Deutz's air-cooled engines range from 87 bhp in-line fours to 400 bhp V-12s. The advantages of air cooling are a shorter warm-up period, which minimises wear, no boiling or freezing problems, fewer accessories and items to go wrong, and lower weight. The absence of a water jacket makes an air-cooled engine slightly noisier than a water-cooled one, but the difference is small when the trucks are on the move.

Many heavy-duty truck engines are in-line units with six cylinders: this offers the best compromise between size, refinement, number of parts, rigidity, and cost. V-engines are useful for retaining parts commonality across a wide horsepower range and for minimum overall dimensions — a V-12 is no longer or deeper than a straight six and need be very little wider; and a V-6 or a straight six with identical cylinder dimensions can easily be developed from it.

Most proprietary engine makers, and indeed some truck makers, offer both in-line and V engines. In general the mainland European and Japanese truck manufacturers build their own engines, whereas in North America only Mack and GMC, and in Britain only Leyland and GMC's subsidiary Bedford, build a high proportion of their own heaviest truck engines (Caterpillar in America also makes engines, but its vehicles are mainly off-road dumpers). This difference in practice is explained by the very much more advanced state of the proprietary engine and components industry in the English-speaking world and the long tradition among truck builders of relying on specialists to supply the equipment.

The major United States proprietary engine makers are Detroit Diesel, Cummins, and Caterpillar. Detroit supplies engines to GMC, Ford, Mack, and also to the main 'assemblers' in North America as well as to Bedford, Scammell, and others in the United Kingdom. Cummins makes probably the most widely used engines for maximum-weight highway trucks and also builds a range of massive dump-truck diesels. All the major U.S. truck makers offer Cummins

Left Cut-away view of a Detroit Diesel 8V-92T unit used in the top-weight version of Bedford's flagship, the TM 4400 tractor for 44-tonne gcw operation. The engine, like almost all Detroit's units, is a two-stroke. Of V8 configuration, it displaces 12.06 litres and develops 394 bhp at 1,950 rpm with turbocharging.

Above Deutz engines are unique among western European and North American heavy road-truck engines in being air-cooled. This BF8L 413F unit, a V8 of 12.76 litres, develops 295 bhp with twin turbocharger and after-cooling. Air-cooling eliminates boiling and freezing problems and, by saving weight, increases payloads.

engines as options, as do ERF, Foden, British Leyland, Ford, Bedford, and Seddon Atkinson in Britain (Cummins has a major production plant in Scotland). Caterpillar offers in-line and V-configuration four-stroke, water-cooled diesels of 175 to 450 bhp that are used by all the big-name North American truck makers.

Deutz is the only major producer of very-large-horsepower proprietary diesels in mainland Europe. Lower down the horsepower range come the German firm MWM and the Perkins company (owned by Massey-Ferguson), whose headquarters are at Peterborough, England. Perkins in fact produces more diesels than any other company in the world, but the bulk of its output is of four- and six-cylinder engines of up to 150 bhp, suitable only for light- and medium-weight trucks. In recent years it has added V-8 engines to its range; these are widely used by makers such as Ford (UK), Leyland, and the Spanish firm Ebro for trucks of up to 28 tonnes gvw. A recent development has been a 10.5-litre V-8 which produces 215 bhp when normally aspirated, 250 bhp when turbocharged, and 290 bhp with turbocharger and after-cooler, and this last version is plainly suitable for maximum-weight trucks.

The other major heavy-truck proprietary-engine makers in Britain are Rolls-Royce and Gardner. Rolls-Royce makes its engines in the old Sentinel truck works at Shrewsbury and has a range broadly similar

to that of Cummins. Its Eagle series of engines runs from 220 to 750 bhp, the latter a 26.1-litre V-12 originally conceived for military purposes and used in de-rated form in the Scammell Commander. Rolls-Royce Motors, which includes the original firm's diesel-engine and luxury-cars divisions, is now owned by Vickers, whose rival in the aeronautics and general engineering field, Hawker Siddeley, has recently bought Gardner, which has made diesels since 1930. Gardner, like Fiat and Mercedes-Benz, has a firm preference for normally aspirated engines, which achieve the same objectives of high and constant torque output as their modern turbocharged 'torque-rise' rivals by dint of meticulous manufacturing methods and high-precision fuel-injection and combustion systems. For example, its 10.5-litre, 200 bhp 6LXB unit has a torque output varying by only 5.3 per cent between 1,000 and 1,920 rpm. Its largest truck engine, the 265 bhp 8LXC, has a capacity of 13.94 litres and is unique among modern diesels in being of straight-eight layout. Gardner engines are renowned for their long and reliable service —more than 1 million miles is commonplace —their low weight, owing to the widespread use of aluminium and magnesium alloys, and their very low fuel consumption, which is equalled only by a few of the latest 'torque-rise' engines. Unfortunately, all these virtues cost money: litre for litre, Gardner diesels are among the most expensive available, but there is no doubt that they are also among the best.

In addition to conventional engines, Rolls-Royce and Gardner make 'flat' engines in which the cylinders are positioned horizontally instead of vertically. Such designs are used today mainly in underfloor-engined buses. During the 1940s and 1950s Sentinel was renowned for its flat-engined trucks, but today the only well-known users of the idea on trucks are FBW in Switzerland (who, despite building less than 200 trucks a year, makes its own 11.95-litre six-cylinder diesels) and MAN's Büssing division. Such engines are located between the axles and between and below the chassis side members. The advantage of such a layout is good accessibility, simpler cab design, excellent unladen-weight distribution, and a low centre of gravity.

So far we have considered only diesel-engined heavy trucks, as this is the type of engine used by virtually all such vehicles. The only notable exceptions are petrol engines used in some US mass-produced trucks of up to 200 bhp and some fire appliances in both Britain (where Rolls-Royce engines were used) and North America. Cost and fuel consumption is of secondary importance in this latter application, and instant starting and the ability to rev freely and accelerate hard are important petrol-engine advantages. The only potential rival to the diesel for normal haulage would appear to be a petrol engine designed to run on a cheaper alternative fuel such as liquefied petroleum gas (LPG), consisting of propane or mixed propane and butane, and several experiments are currently under way. For military purposes, multi-fuel engines able to run on everything from aviation fuel to peanut oil, and using spark or compression ignition as alternatives, are already in production.

Until the price of fuel rocketed upward in the 1970s it seemed likely that the gas turbine would be the heavy-truck power unit of the future. The gas turbine is basically a jet driving a very-high-speed turbine that can be geared down for use with a conventional transmission. It was found to be unsuited to stop/start operation as there was a distinct time lag between moving from idle to its operating speed of 40,000 rpm or more. However, when it was used intensively at close to maximum power, as in long-distance trucking,

its consumption was found to be comparable to a diesel's, once efficient heat exchangers had been developed to convert the units' waste exhaust-heat energy into usable power.

Although gas turbines are widely used for other purposes (notably in aviation, railways, and shipping), they were not persevered with in the truck field as their manufacturing costs are far higher than those of a comparable diesel. The price of such units could have been brought down only by semi-mass production, and as operators were not prepared to re-equip their maintenance shops or re-train their staff it seemed unlikely that an economic sales volume would ever be achieved. As a result MAN, GM, Leyland, and others quietly shelved their research into gas turbines.

Electricity is the only other possibility at present, but until storage methods can be lightened and cheapened, battery-powered traction will be limited to the light local-delivery vehicle. In the meantime work continues on so-called hybrid prototypes, which have small diesel-engined generators topping-up the batteries while the truck is at work on the road.

Below Autocar Construcktor 2 showing engine accessibility when its glass-fibre hood is hinged open. A short-bonnet conventional, with engine over the front axle and partly within the cab, this KS cab has a BBC of only 2,490 mm (98 in). Proprietary diesels ranging from 210 to 430 bhp can be specified.

Right A typical forward-control cab of the mid-1970s: a White Freightliner fully tilted, showing its massive Caterpillar 3408 diesel, which develops 450 bhp. Extra BBC length due to sleeper compartment makes it difficult to remove the engine from chassis when major repairs become necessary.

Transmission and braking

For the foreseeable future, then, it will be the diesel-engined truck that dominates heavy transport, and we must now consider how it transmits its power to the road. First comes the clutch, which nowadays is normally a twin-plate design to give the largest possible friction-lining area, and has air/hydraulic actuation and automatic adjustment. We have already seen how the modern 'torque-rise' engine can be mated to a gearbox with relatively few ratios — six to eight being commonplace for normal conditions. However, in several parts of the world more arduous conditions prevail, as on North America's west coast or on the Alpine passes of Europe. In such conditions a typical gearbox may not have sufficient ratios to keep the engine 'on the cam' (at peak-torque speed) and maintain a high average road speed.

A common way around this on medium-weight trucks is to fit a two-speed axle, which can be switched from high to low ratio on the move to effectively double the number of gearbox ratios. The same principle is applied in the modern splitter gearboxes used on the heavy trucks, although the splits occur in the box (the splitter is normally mounted on the front of it) and not at the axle. A splitter gearbox with, say, five basic ratios can be driven as a simple

feature of the Road Ranger is its use of twin countershafts, which split the input torque from the engine. This enables smaller shafts to be used, and reduces the bearing loads.

There are two distinct schools of thought about synchromesh on heavy-truck constant-mesh gearboxes. In general, mainland European firms are in favour of it; for example, the 16-speed range-change Mercedes-Benz gearbox has it, as do almost all Volvo and Scania gearboxes. British, North American, and Japanese heavy truck makers tend to favour constant-mesh gearboxes without synchronisers, regarding them as more robust and straightforward, with less to go wrong and much lighter as well. Most experienced drivers, too, prefer the positive feel to the slightly baulking action of synchromesh. Synchro allows less-precise gear changes, when engine revs are not matched perfectly to roadspeed before meshing; but all heavy-truck drivers are professionals, and soon get used to the

Eaton-Fuller Road Ranger gearboxes come in various types, but all have twin countershafts to split torque loadings. The type shown here is the 13-speed box. The main flange for the propeller shaft is on the left, with two power-takeoff flanges on either side of it. Above the lower one is an air-operated piston that actuates the range-change, giving four extra forward ratios.

five-speeder when the truck is unladen. But for heavy loads any or all gears can be 'split' (that is, given a different ratio — usually higher, as a lower one might overload the gears) to give up to 10 ratios. Alternatively or additionally is the range-change box. In a gearbox with a five-speed main section the driver uses each of the five in turn, then he operates the 'range-change' switch and goes through the gears again in the same order but now in a different ratio.

Sixteen and occasionally even more ratios can be provided by such range-change gearboxes as the Eaton-Fuller Road Ranger. On the Ford Transcontinental this consists of a five forward speed and reverse main section with an air-operated range-change at the rear operating on the four upper gears (first gear being a 'crawler' ratio). This gives nine speeds, which are boosted to 13 by a close-ratio splitter overdrive gear on the top four high-range gears. Not so long ago, on some trucks this would have involved using two gear-shift levers, but now all functions are on one and this greatly simplifies driving. A

more accurate changes required without synchro. In any case, typical ratio steps of only about 300 rpm are relatively easy to match.

If many of today's truck engines are proprietary units, an even higher proportion of the gearboxes they use is built by specialists. The industry is dominated by United States companies, notably Eaton (which also owns Fuller), Dana (which also owns Spicer and Turner), Allison, and Clark. The only other firm with wide international ramifications is ZF (Zahnradfabrik Friedrichshafen) of West Germany.

An option on some heavy trucks used for site work is a torque converter in addition to the normal gearbox. Volvo, Foden, Fiat, Scammell, Scania, and others offer such vehicles, which have the advantage of clutchless changes and greatly increased torque at low speed. Dump-trucks often use torque converters in conjunction with automatic gear boxes. General Motor's Allison subsidiary and ZF are perhaps the best-known makers of automatic gearboxes.

Automatic gearboxes are widely used on special-purpose vehicles

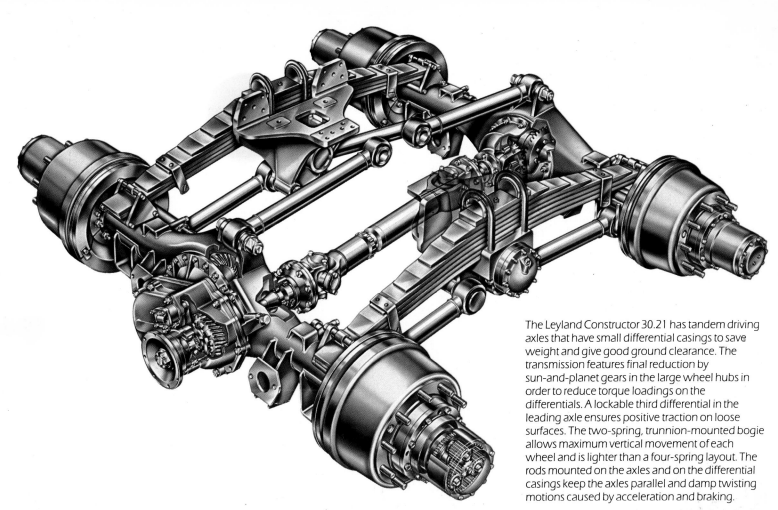

The Leyland Constructor 30.21 has tandem driving axles that have small differential casings to save weight and give good ground clearance. The transmission features final reduction by sun-and-planet gears in the large wheel hubs in order to reduce torque loadings on the differentials. A lockable third differential in the leading axle ensures positive traction on loose surfaces. The two-spring, trunnion-mounted bogie allows maximum vertical movement of each wheel and is lighter than a four-spring layout. The rods mounted on the axles and on the differential casings keep the axles parallel and damp twisting motions caused by acceleration and braking.

like garbage collectors, but for normal haulage they are not in favour because they raise fuel consumption and do not give the driver the total control provided by a manual system. Most automatic gearboxes have built-in retarders that slow the vehicle when the driver takes his foot off the accelerator; but these do not give quite the reassurance on a long descent that judicious gearbox down-changes can. On the other hand, a lot of the prejudice against 'automatics' is unfounded, and they seem likely to become more common, if only as a means of cushioning vehicles against transmission shock in urban driving.

Retarders are also used on some manual-gearbox trucks not only to save the brake linings but to increase total braking efficiency. One type converts energy into magnetic or hydraulic resistance to rotation of the propeller shaft. Caterpillar's BrakeSaver, actuated automatically and/or manually, is hydraulic and uses the braking effect set up when oil is picked up by a crankshaft-driven rotor wheel and thrown against the fins of a stationary stator wheel. The more oil that is pumped into the retarder, the greater is the braking effect. Another type, called an exhaust brake, works by altering the timing of the opening and closing of the exhaust valves in the combustion chambers. This has the effect of building up pressure, which prevents fresh gases from entering the chambers.

The normal service brakes on the heavier trucks are usually actuated by a compressed-air system, but some medium-weight models have air-over-hydraulic systems in which the air simply gives pressurised assistance to the conventional hydraulics, which resemble those fitted to ordinary cars. Most full-air systems have a fail-safe system known as a spring brake. This consists of a heavy duty spring that is compressed by air pressure when the engine is running and the system is working normally. But if the air pressure fails or the engine stops, the spring closes and automatically applies the brakes. An added refinement is load-sensing valves which relate the amount of pressure applied to the brakes to the load on the wheels; without such valves there is a tendency for the braked wheels to lock when a truck is unladen — and this is not only an inefficient way to stop but can be dangerous. Except on dumptrucks, brakes on the top-weight trucks are usually of the drum type, which are easier and cheaper to

maintain than discs; though developments of the latter type, made by Goodrich in North America, and Girling and Perrot in Europe, are being offered as a way of saving weight.

As we have seen, many heavy trucks, and artic tractors especially, have more than one driven axle. If two are driven, the rearmost is powered either by a tailshaft from the first axle, or else is connected directly to its own prop shaft by an additional shaft routed over the first axle. In either case some form of torque proportioner ensures the correct amount of power is delivered to each axle.

Chassis and suspension

All the components considered so far are built as lightly as durability and strength will allow. The same goes for the chassis, though extra strength and rigidity here may mean that other components do not have to be built to withstand flexing, twisting, and vibration. Aluminium alloy is a high-cost way of achieving this objective of strength with lightness, and aluminium-framed trucks have been made since the 1930s, mainly in North America, but also in France, Switzerland, and Britain (the Jensen was a pioneer in 1939, having a chassis made from hiduminium tubes). In 1958 Autocar, by using chassis, radiator tanks, and wheels made from aluminium along with a glass-fibre cab trimmed no less than 1,905 kg (4,200 lb) from the weight of its 6 x 4 conventional tractor. Since then many other components made from lightweight materials have been added to the standard or optional specification of U.S. trucks. For the 1980 model season, Chevrolet managed to remove a further 225 kg (495 lb) of deadweight from its Titan three-axle cab-over trucks, and manufacturers around the world are working on ways of shifting deadweight into extra payload. Steel chassis members are usually tapered so that only the points that actually take the bulk of the strain are of full depth. Some have drawn-steel side members which are thicker on the flanges than on the web; others have an extra flitched section where the weight falls, as in the centre and rear of a tipper.

Another area of saving or compromise concerns suspension. Highly sophisticated systems add unnecessary expense and weight and do little for a laden vehicle. Where they score is in improving driver comfort (to some extent this is already catered for by

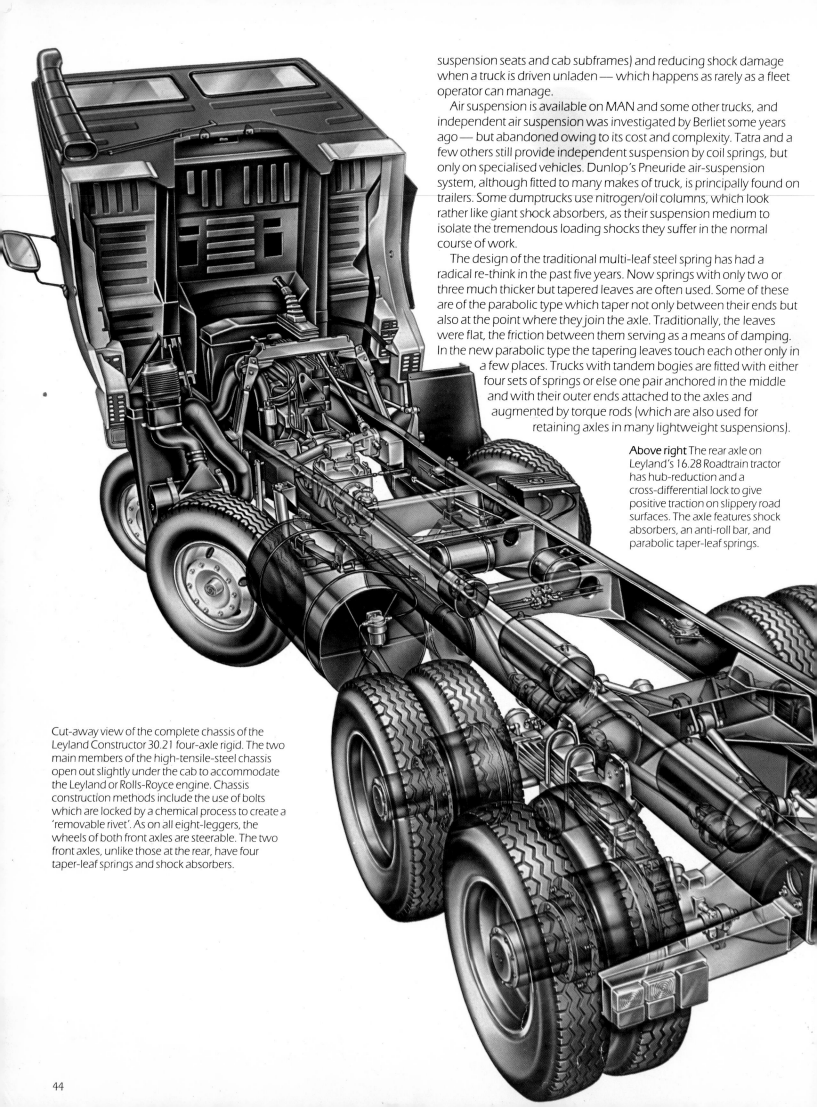

suspension seats and cab subframes) and reducing shock damage when a truck is driven unladen — which happens as rarely as a fleet operator can manage.

Air suspension is available on MAN and some other trucks, and independent air suspension was investigated by Berliet some years ago — but abandoned owing to its cost and complexity. Tatra and a few others still provide independent suspension by coil springs, but only on specialised vehicles. Dunlop's Pneuride air-suspension system, although fitted to many makes of truck, is principally found on trailers. Some dumptrucks use nitrogen/oil columns, which look rather like giant shock absorbers, as their suspension medium to isolate the tremendous loading shocks they suffer in the normal course of work.

The design of the traditional multi-leaf steel spring has had a radical re-think in the past five years. Now springs with only two or three much thicker but tapered leaves are often used. Some of these are of the parabolic type which taper not only between their ends but also at the point where they join the axle. Traditionally, the leaves were flat, the friction between them serving as a means of damping. In the new parabolic type the tapering leaves touch each other only in a few places. Trucks with tandem bogies are fitted with either four sets of springs or else one pair anchored in the middle and with their outer ends attached to the axles and augmented by torque rods (which are also used for retaining axles in many lightweight suspensions).

Above right The rear axle on Leyland's 16.28 Roadtrain tractor has hub-reduction and a cross-differential lock to give positive traction on slippery road surfaces. The axle features shock absorbers, an anti-roll bar, and parabolic taper-leaf springs.

Cut-away view of the complete chassis of the Leyland Constructor 30.21 four-axle rigid. The two main members of the high-tensile-steel chassis open out slightly under the cab to accommodate the Leyland or Rolls-Royce engine. Chassis construction methods include the use of bolts which are locked by a chemical process to create a 'removable rivet'. As on all eight-leggers, the wheels of both front axles are steerable. The two front axles, unlike those at the rear, have four taper-leaf springs and shock absorbers.

This system allows maximum articulation for tippers and the like. Foden is an advocate of rubber suspension on the back of tippers, which it claims saves weight and maintenance time as well as obviating costly spring breakages —— the bane of site-vehicle operators. Such vehicles with two driven axles, incidentally, usually have lockable differentials, including an 'inter-axle differential', to ensure maximum traction in tricky conditions.

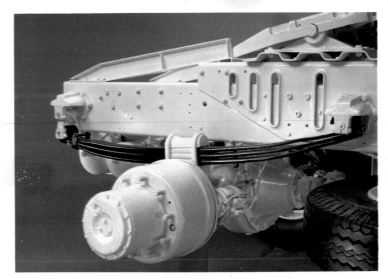

Power-assisted steering is pretty well universal on top-weight trucks, as are power-assisted controls for the clutch and brakes. Power-steering design is absolutely critical on artics as the driver has to retain complete 'feel' of the outfit to avoid jack-knifing. Usually it is arranged to give very light assistance around the dead-ahead position, with real power being fed in only for low-speed, maximum-lock manoeuvrability. Various types of anti-jack-knife devices have been invented over the years. Most of them involve the use of frictional dampers incorporated into the fifth-wheel.

The quest for economy

An important refinement which is often required by operators of premium-specification vehicles is automatic chassis lubrication. In such a system all the vital greasing points are linked by pipe to a

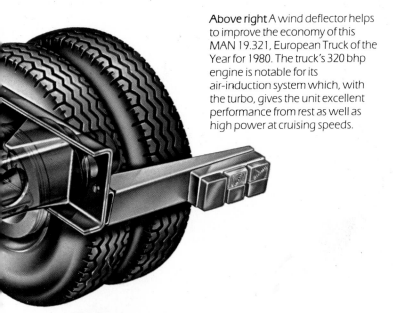

Above right A wind deflector helps to improve the economy of this MAN 19.321, European Truck of the Year for 1980. The truck's 320 bhp engine is notable for its air-induction system which, with the turbo, gives the unit excellent performance from rest as well as high power at cruising speeds.

special pump and lubricant dispenser, which operates at a predetermined moment — for example, every time the clutch pedal is depressed. Although relatively expensive, automatic chassis lubrication may more than repay its cost by lengthening the life of components and reducing the amount of time a truck has to be off the road for servicing.

With fuel saving becoming an important priority, all sorts of developments are finding their way into production vehicles. Both as a means of saving fuel and to ensure rapid engine warm-up (thus preventing excessive wear before lubricating oil has fully circulated), the automatic radiator shutter of the Kysor type has become popular. It is more effective than the usual thermostatic valve fitted between engine and radiator and can at least be seen to be working. Its own thermostat ensures that the engine reaches optimum temperature rapidly and then stays exactly there. Another way of achieving this is the variable-pitch or the viscous fan. The ordinary cooling fan runs all the time, whether needed or not, and absorbs up to 5 bhp from the engine. By working only when it is actually needed, the fan saves fuel and also does a more efficient job of keeping the coolant water at optimum temperature. The variable-pitch fan has its blades feathered by a thermostat, while the drive to the viscous fan can vary between slipping and total engagement, depending on temperature.

Another valuable way of saving fuel is by reducing a truck's wind resistance and turbulence. Big strides have been made in aerodynamics (or 'wind management', as some truck stylists insist on

calling it) by smoothing the contours of the modern cab and reducing its overall height, as on the Leyland Roadtrain and 'New Generation' Mercedes-Benz. But there is no point in having a 'slippery' cab if behind it sits a higher, box-section, wind-catching trailer. Many trailers now have rounded 'foreheads' to improve wind flow, but this does not cure the eddying that takes place, especially between the cab and semi-trailer of an artic. Over the past few years wind-tunnel tests have been used to devise the ideal shape of a wind deflector that can be attached to the cab roof to act as an efficient spoiler. Fuel savings of up to 15 per cent are claimed from the use of scientifically designed deflectors — but the common practice of leaving them upright even when not towing a high trailer must negate most of the gains. The truck of the future seems likely to have a built-in adjustable spoiler; it may be used to form the front wall for an over-cab sleeping compartment, as on the White Windstreamer.

More and more components will be made of aluminium alloy and new lightweight materials like carbon fibre, already used in some propeller shafts. Transmission power losses will be reduced and engines will have ever more sophisticated fuel-metering devices and air-induction systems to save fuel and increase torque. The life expectancy of chassis should increase with improved materials and techniques — and already the life of heavy US trucks is lengthened by buying complete 'glider kits', which update worn out vehicles by replacing all the major mechanical units at the front of a chassis with a ready-assembled 'half' truck. The next 10 years should see as many dramatic developments as in all the previous 80 years of truck evolution.

THE HEAVY TRUCK
WORLD LEADERS

The heavy-truck industry world-wide has seen dramatic changes in the past 20 years. Although total production has greatly increased, a large number of firms have been absorbed by stronger national or international competitors, or have simply disappeared.

Western Europe

In this major market one important alternative to takeovers has been commercial agreements involving technical cooperation — and these have tended to cross national frontiers as if they did not exist.

IVECO (Industrial Vehicles Corporation) is perhaps the prime example of international takeovers. Its formation was master-minded by Fiat, which, over the years, had already taken over its major Italian competitors — OM in 1933 and Lancia in 1969. In 1966 it had acquired control of Unic, the large and old-established French truck maker previously owned by Simca.

In 1975 IVECO was formed when Fiat's commercial and truck interests were merged with Magirus Deutz. Fiat owned 80 per cent of the stock in the new company, the rest being held by Magirus Deutz's parent, Klöckner-Humboldt-Deutz (KHD) of Ulm. Fiat has now acquired KHD's share; Magirus builds trucks for IVECO, while KHD concentrates on building the highly regarded Deutz air-cooled diesel engines and agricultural tractors. As well as its range of all-wheel-drive off-road vehicles and fire appliances, Magirus brought to IVECO a new medium-weight range developed since 1971, when the firm had formed ETD (European Truck Development group, commonly known as the 'Club of Four') with Volvo, DAF, and SAVIEM.

IVECO vehicles are made or assembled in 26 countries around the world, and outside Europe the group is particularly strong in Africa and South America. It makes some 250 basic models with engines developing up to 360 bhp; over 35,000 heavy vehicles were made in 1977, when the group accounted for 87.2 per cent of trucks sold in Italy, 15.1 in France, 15.9 in Germany, 16.9 in Switzerland, and 23 in the EEC as a whole.

Spain and Switzerland's truck industries provide a contrast in fortunes since World War II. In Spain, where the market is dominated by three indigenous firms, there has been considerable penetration by overseas companies: Pegaso (formed in 1946 as successor to famed Hispano-Suiza) is mainly state-owned, but International Harvester has recently acquired a minority stake in the company; Barreiros, founded in 1958, was bought from Chrysler in 1978 by Peugeot-Citroën and its trucks are now marketed under the Dodge label; Ebro, which made trucks based on Ford (UK) parts until 1956, was acquired by Massey-Ferguson and is now partly owned by Nissan.

In Switzerland the several firms of heavy-truck builders have all managed so far to resist overtures from foreign rivals. The largest and best-known is Saurer, of Arbon, founded in 1903, which in 1929 took over the other major truck builder, Berna. Until the end of the 1970s Saurer marketed virtually identical heavy trucks under both names; recently, however, the firm has abandoned the Berna name.

Saurer was very early into the diesel field, and was offering a range of diesel-powered trucks by 1928. Saurer produces less than 1,000 heavy trucks a year; they are extremely expensive but are undoubtedly among the world's best in design, construction, and performance. Almost as highly regarded in their own field are two much smaller firms, FBW and Mowag. In spite of relatively tiny annual production, both firms build many of their own engines, FBW being responsible for a series of notable horizontal underfloor units since 1949, and Mowag developing turbocharged multi-fuel units.

France now has only Unic (IVECO-owned), Peugeot-Citroën — which makes Dodge in Britain and Spain, but no heavy trucks on

Pages 46-7 A White Western Star of about 1970. White has had a very difficult past decade with mounting losses and a number of abortive take-over bids.

Left A Fiat 190F 35 drawbar-trailer reefer outfit on an Alpine motorway. Owner of OM and Lancia, and Unic of France, Fiat also controls IVECO, which includes Magirus.

French soil — and the state-owned Renault. Of these the most important in the heavy-truck field is Renault, which controls Berliet (founded in 1902) and SAVIEM (1955) and is in the process of integrating the Renault name. SAVIEM (Société Anonyme de Véhicules Industriels et d'Équipments Mécaniques) was formed out of three truck firms bought by Renault; its recent technical links have been with MAN and the Club of Four. Berliet joined Renault in 1975 after eight rather unsuccessful years under Citroën ownership.

The largest SAVIEM-derived Renaults still owe much to equivalent MAN trucks, but the Berliets are virtually all designed and made under 'one roof'. They feature the Maxicouple engine, which is very similar to the 'Big Cam' Cummins and to the Mack and Leyland 'torque-rise' engines. The largest forward-control Berliet cab is basically identical to that used by Ford Europe on its Amsterdam-built Transcontinental models; a luxury version of this cab, with raised and streamlined roof, is used as the top 360 bhp Renault.

West Germany, too, has seen a dramatic contraction in the number of its heavy-truck firms. Specialists like Kaelble and Faun are mentioned elsewhere; which leaves only MAN, Mercedes-Benz, and Magirus. Mercedes absorbed the famous heavy-truck maker Hanomag-Henschel in 1969, acquired the Euclid dumptruck firm from White in 1977, has numerous links with other manufacturers — notably in Austria (Steyr) and eastern Europe — and truck-assembly plants in Argentina, Brazil, the United States (Virginia), India, Saudi Arabia, and elsewhere. It makes virtually everything that goes into its vehicles and is technically very advanced. As far as is possible the models use interchangeable parts, so that most spares for, say, one of its V-8 engines will also fit its V-10 units and vice versa. To have the very latest technology and to share expense, some engine-design work is shared with MAN and the two have a joint company called MTU making outsize diesel engines for dumptrucks, railway locomotives, and the like.

Like Fiat, Mercedes-Benz seems anxious to stick to normally aspirated engines wherever possible, hence the massive 14.6-litre units in its big tractors, although its latest top-weight truck, the 1638, uses a turbocharged version of this engine. The 'New Generation' modular forward-control cab, in various guises, fits most of the range, is aerodynamically efficient, and helps reduce production costs. With

Below Mercedes-Benz is Europe's largest truck builder and a major exporter. This 6 x 4 with 'New Generation' cab is built to Australian spec., with V-10 diesel, sleeper, air conditioning, roof-mounted air cleaner, and anti-kangaroo 'roo-bar' mounted over the front bumper.

Right above Successors to this TR280 and other Berliet models will have the Renault badge; the latter firm bought Berliet in 1975.

Right below Magirus is known for its rugged site vehicles and builds this eight-legger specially for the UK.

a share of about half the heavy trucks in West Germany and major exports, Mercedes-Benz is the largest heavy-truck maker in Europe.

Its great rival is MAN (first trucks in 1915) which, until its 1979 agreement to make joint MAN-Volkswagen light-to-medium trucks, was solely a top-weight truck maker (it bought out big-truck specialist Büssing in 1971). Like Mercedes it was one of the diesel pioneers and has consistently been responsible for important theoretical and practical research on the subject (it built the world's first V-8 diesel in 1951). Much of its knowhow is used under licence by diesel-truck manufacturers around the world, and MAN has particularly strong ties with manufacturers in communist Europe. An associate in Austria, ÖAF, makes some of its largest models, including 6 x 4 and 6 x 6 Jumbo site vehicles and heavy-haulage tractors, as well as 8 x 8 military trucks for NATO forces.

The Netherlands and Belgium have seen the rise since World War II of several small firms making heavy on/off-road trucks such as tippers. These include the Belgian MOL and the Dutch FTF, Ginaf, RAM, and Terberg. But, internationally, by far the most important truck builder in the Benelux countries is DAF (Van Doornes Automobielfabriecken), whose predecessor was founded at Eindhoven in 1928 to make trailers. It began to concentrate on trucks immediately after World War II, initially using Leyland components and expertise, but after the early 1960s DAF emerged as a manufacturer in its own right. It has developed a range of efficient diesel engines which have a very high power-to-weight ratio owing to a relatively small swept capacity and highly sophisticated fuel-injection and combustion-chamber design. Typical is its 2800 range of six-cylinder engines, which develop up to 307 bhp from a modest 11.6 litres. In 1972 DAF disposed of its car division to Volvo in order to concentrate solely on trucks, and today it is one-third-owned by International Harvester.

Undoubtedly the stars of the European heavy-vehicle industry in recent years have been the Scandinavians. Sisu (founded 1931) is little known outside its native Finland, but it relies to a considerable extent on Britain for its engines, Rolls-Royce and Leyland being major component suppliers. A minority interest in Sisu is held by both Leyland and Scania.

If Sisu caters mainly for the Finnish market, Scania (1903) and Volvo (1928) in neighbouring Sweden are very much geared to world markets. They were little known outside Scandinavia until 20 years ago; but at the beginning of the 1960s all the European operators wanted big-horsepower trucks to cope with the new higher permitted weights and increased long-distance operations. Sweden was already using such machines and they had the added attractions of excellent engineering, strong, well-insulated cabs, many years of experience of turbocharging (pioneered by Volvo and by MAN in the early 1950s), and, to suit the environmental lobby, very quiet engines.

Scania and Volvo took the European industry by storm; they were particularly successful in Britain, which was one of the last countries to modernise its road-haulage system. The two firms now have large shares of the maximum-weight truck market in most European countries (Volvo has the largest individual share in Britain, helped by its large assembly plant in Scotland), and are expanding their influence in the Middle East, Australia, Africa, North America (where Volvo is distributed by Freightliner), and South America.

Like DAF in Holland, Scania and Volvo believe in making small engines work very hard for their living. This contradicts U.S. and British experience, which suggests that large, lightly stressed engines last longer and are more economical. However, with the use of top-grade materials engineered to the most exacting tolerances, the Scandinavian engines work well and use fuel sparingly, even if they do not offer maximum torque over such a wide rev. band as do the latest 'torque-rise' units, which drivers in some countries prefer.

After it joined the international league in the early 1960s Volvo made a staggering 135,000 of its F85/6/8 models before these were replaced by the even better F7/10/12 models in 1977-8. Latest Volvo flagship is the Globetrotter, a luxury version of the F12 with a trailer, better-equipped cab and 385 bhp engine. Scania's current top-of-the-range is the 142H tractor, whose 14.2-litre V-8 turbo develops higher torque than any of its European rivals bar Fiat's massive 17-litre engine in turbocharged form.

Until Scandinavia became a major source of heavy trucks, Britain was one of the world's most successful producers. The British industry was caught on the hop in the late 1960s and early 1970s by uncertainty as to whether the UK would be joining the EEC and/or whether its weight limits would be harmonised with the rest of western Europe. It took until the late 1970s for Britain's truck firms to

Left A MAN 38-tonne gtw truck with tri-axle semi for TIR work. Famed for engineering innovation ever since it pioneered truck diesels, MAN in recent years has greatly increased its earnings by selling advanced technology abroad, especially to truck builders in eastern Europe.

Below Like its Scandinavian rivals, DAF has a reputation for technical excellence and aggressive export selling, and it has sold more than 10,000 heavy trucks to Britain in the past 15 years or so. This UK-registered tanker is drawn by DAF's FT2300 tractor, which is powered by an 8.25-litre, straight-six, 230 bhp unit with turbo.

come to grips with the new situation, but they are now poised to take the technical initiative once more. Unfortunately, during the period of transition many firms ran into financial crises and were rescued only by American intervention. Thus Seddon and Atkinson, who had merged in 1970 for added security and to pool their resources in the production of the advanced 200/300/400 range, hit difficulties before the results could be seen and were snapped up by International Harvester in 1974. Both Atkinson and Seddon had been primarily assemblers, although Seddon did have a drive-axle production facility. The Seddon Atkinson heavies continue to use proprietary engines; its top-of-the-range 401 model, powered by a Cummins turbo, is a notably lightweight tractor making extensive use of SMC and aluminium.

Britain has, indeed, been a second home to the big North American firms, and Ford and General Motors (through its Vauxhall/Bedford subsidiary) treat Britain as their major truck-producing country outside North America. Both their European truck ranges have recently moved into the top-weight category. The biggest Ford, the Transcontinental, comes not from Britain but from Amsterdam, although it uses British-made Cummins engines. The largest British-built Fords (for 28 tons gcw) use Cummins and Perkins engines. Ford's own turbocharged six-cylinder engines now develop up to about 150 bhp.

The top-of-the-range Bedford TM uses GM's own UK-built in-line, six-cylinder, four-stroke diesel of 150 bhp and Detroit Diesel two-stroke V-6 or V-8 or Cummins four-stroke, straight sixes for the heavier-weight models. The largest versions of the TM and Transcontinental are both 6 x 4 tractors units capable of up to 44 tonnes gcw operation in mainland Europe (or even higher weights where permissible).

Above New for 1981 was the Seddon Atkinson 401 tractor, a lightweight version of the 400. With much polished aluminium, the big Atki reflects the marketing policies of the firm's American owner, International Harvester.

Right Volvo N10.33 6 x 4 at work on a harbour project in Dubai. Many truck operators in the Third World favour normal-control cabs, and Leyland, DAF, Magirus, MAN, Berliet, and Volvo all build heavy tractors of this design for export.

Perhaps unluckiest of the European heavy-truck manufacturers in the 1970s was Foden. One of the last of the relatively small firms (outside Switzerland) to make the bulk of its own components, and with an output of about 40 trucks a week including dumpers (of which it was one of the major producers), it had the lion's share of the eight-wheeler-rigid market in Britain and had won big orders for its high-mobility trucks for NATO. On the strength of all this it embarked on an expansion programme to treble production.

Although it had stopped making its own two-stroke truck engines in the 1960s, it now found that it could not make other major parts as cheaply as its competitors could buy them in from specialists. It decided then to wind down its own component-manufacturing facilities and offer a range of assembled trucks instead, notably the Haulmaster and the top-weight Fleetmaster for 38-tonne gcw operation. The products were good, but the market had taken a downturn; market sectors that previously had been dominated by Foden were now being strenuously fought over by importers of foreign trucks desperate to break into what appeared at the time to be perhaps the last truly open heavy-truck market left in Europe. Foden never came anywhere near its new production targets and, working continually at under capacity, never made any money with its new range. The firm came near to bankruptcy, was nearly nationalised and

then almost taken over by Rolls-Royce. Finally, in 1980, the money ran out again and Foden was acquired by the American PACCAR group, which owns Kenworth, Peterbilt, and Dart. As their prize, Paccar gained control of one of the most modern heavy-truck assembly plants in the world and a company name renowned for its quality products since the earliest days of the road truck.

Leyland is, of course, the major British truck and bus producer. The parent company first made internal-combustion-engined trucks in 1904, but its great expansion began in 1951 with the acquisition of Albion (founded in 1902); since then many other famous names have been absorbed —Thornycroft (which made its first truck in 1896), AEC (1912), Guy (1914), Scammell (1919), Aveling-Barford (amalgamated 1933), and BMC (formed from Austin and Morris's truck divisions in 1955). Of these the only names to survive on heavy trucks, apart from Leyland, are Scammell and Aveling-Barford, most of whose vehicles are highly specialised. Leyland, like White, has found that construction-machinery and dumptruck manufacture is less compatible with heavy-truck building than might be supposed, and in 1980 it was trying to sell Aveling-Barford as a going concern. About the only 'regular-production' heavy trucks that Scammell produces in its Watford factory are the bonneted S series and the Leyland Constructor rigid eight-wheeler chassis.

The true Leylands are split between the Scottish-built models which go up to the Perkins V-8-powered Mastiff 28-tonner and the trucks made at Leyland, Lancashire. Top of these is the new Roadtrain, part of the T45 series, which incorporates all the latest technical refinements and has been highly acclaimed. It uses Leyland's own 12.5-litre Flexitorque TL12 straight-six engine developing 270 bhp, or Cummins or Rolls-Royce proprietary units. Many of its components, including the cab, are common to the Constructor and in time will give 60 per cent parts commonality between a whole range of 6.5- to 65-tonne models. Another new-generation Leyland is the Landtrain normal-control range made in the former Guy factory at Wolverhampton and aimed primarily at overseas markets. It uses Leyland or Cummins engines of 212 to 290 bhp and is intended for arduous operation and easy maintenance. Leyland has assembly plants or associates around the world, some of which make trucks specific to local requirements, as in India, Turkey, and Nigeria.

Last, but certainly not least, of the major, wholly-British heavy-truck makers is ERF, whose concept since foundation in 1933 has always been to assemble highly competitive trucks from the best and usually lightest proprietary components available. Its premium specification B-series of four, six, and eight wheelers was launched in 1974 and has been gradually modified, improved, and updated ever since. In its latest 'Super B' form as a 36-tonne gcw tractor, it has shed another 508 kg (½ ton) of unladen weight to get down to a remarkable wet (that is, with fuel and water) unladen weight of 5.48 tonne. ERF is keeping a large new Welsh assembly plant on ice until the world economy, of which the truck is an extremely sensitive barometer, improves. Meanwhile its factory —— virtually next door to Foden's in Sandbach, Cheshire —— is probably the largest producer of maximum-weight trucks in Britain. It has significant overseas markets, notably in Belgium and in South Africa.

Eastern Europe

Until the last few years most of the heavy road trucks in the Soviet Union and its eastern European satellites were civilian versions of military trucks, and the transport network was served mainly by very robust and basic trucks of under 10 tonnes capacity. Fuel shortages, however, and the experience gained by Communist Bloc operators and drivers in western Europe are bringing about changes.

Ford's Transcontinental, built in Amsterdam, was launched in 1975 and has become popular with owner-drivers. The tractors, of which 4 x 2 and 6 x 4 versions are available, are powered by Cummins turbocharged E-series engines developing 240 to 345 bhp. The semi-trailer shown here has a typical TIR-approved cover, which can be rolled back for loading and closed by a wire running through eyelets all the way around the trailer to a customs seal.

Right Flanked on the right by a Scania LB141, and on the left by a mid-1970s Volvo F88, is a Rába 38-tonne rigid plus drawbar-trailer outfit from Hungary. The factory built its first truck in 1904; today, as is evident from this model, Rába uses a lot of MAN technology under licence.

Below The Foden S10 Haulmaster concrete mixer (powered by Gardner diesel) makes extensive use of aluminium and glass-fibre in its lightweight cab, and has maintenance-free rubber rear suspension. Acquired by the American PACCAR group in 1980, the Foden factory now trades as Sandbach Engineering although the trucks retain the famous name.

Poland, Romania, Hungary, Yugoslavia, and Czechoslovakia have acquired some of the latest heavy-truck technology by buying licences from western manufacturers to make complete vehicles or important components. As a result Zastava of Yugoslavia is Fiat-based, while TAM from the same country has had close ties with Magirus since 1957. Jelcz of Poland has used Leyland, Berliet, and Mercedes-Benz features; and several manufacturers build trucks embodying MAN patents, notably Rába of Hungary (originally founded in 1904) and the Romanian Roman.

Czechoslovakia has the most advanced heavy-truck industry in the Communist world. The LIAZ, made at Jablonec-nad-Nisou, embodies most of the modern features of its western competitors and uses a British turbocharger to extract 350 bhp from the 12-litre, six-cylinder engine used in its largest models. A sister make to LIAZ is Tatra, which has been a distinguished name in car and truck design since 1919 but now concentrates mainly on heavy-haulage tractors, site tippers, and military vehicles. These have some unusual features, including independent suspension, backbone chassis, and air-cooled engines. No doubt Tatra would have been forced to comply with the mainstream of heavy-vehicle design if it had been competing in a free market, but as the only producer of trucks for specialised requirements in its own country it has been able to retain and develop the features laid down in the 1920s by its brilliant designer Hans Ledwinka.

Most of the Soviet Union's trucks are antiquated by Western standards and less-advanced than those of its Communist neighbours. The only models to be seen regularly in western Europe are the KRAZ 6 x 4 dump trucks (marketed as BELAZ in Britain), which seem to owe a considerable debt to the American Diamond T Model 980 of World War II (still happily around in large numbers as heavy wreckers). Many of Russia's other trucks, such as the MAZ, GAZ, and ZIL, also have obvious American origins and several are powered by V-8 petrol engines of typical 1950s American vintage.

During the early 1970s the Soviet government called in Ford of America to lay out a factory and help with the design and production of a modern top-weight truck. When the project was well under way the two parties fell out, and the KAMAZ, which emerged in 1978, shows no obvious Ford ancestry but, instead, an amalgam of features from many of the world's major makes. It has a V-8, 210 bhp diesel, a forward-control tilt cab, and is typically a 6 x 4 tractive unit for 35 tonnes gcw or a 6 x 4 rigid for 23 tonnes gvw. It was envisaged that 150,000 KAMAZ would be built in the first year of full production (1980). It seems unlikely that this target was met, but it could well be that the model is produced in larger numbers than any other heavy truck in the world.

North America

The traditional makers of top-weight highway trucks have been faced with competition in recent years from many of the mass-produced medium-weight truck builders. The new breed of heavy truck from the mass-producers is invariably built to a premium specification, and, because sales volumes are relatively low, it is often just as expensive as the specialised hand-built truck. Ford and General Motors now offer ranges of vehicles in North America that give customers the choice of a one-make fleet from smallest delivery van up to giant highway hauler.

Under the skin, the big Fords are much the same as any of the 'assembled' U.S. trucks, offering a choice of the same proprietary engines, axles, gearboxes, and so on, and claiming individuality mainly through the styling of the cabs. The same applies to the GMC except that there the proprietary engine frequently specified (and used by much of the rest of the industry including arch-rival Ford) is made by a GM subsidiary — Detroit Diesels. Ford and GMC have now expanded into a similar field in Europe, where the British-built Bedford TM, with Detroit or Cummins engines, and the Cummins-powered, Dutch-built Ford Transcontinental vie for sales with the might of the European truck industry.

Apart from having its own diesel-engine company, General Motors owns a sizeable part of the Japanese truck maker Isuzu, which supplies it with some smaller diesel engines and makes trucks for certain countries (notably Australia) under the Bedford name. An unusual facet of General Motors was its Terex earthmoving-machinery division until 1980, when it sold the firm to the German construction machinery group IBH. Terex is a relatively recent name (derived in 1969 from **terre,** French for earth, and **rex,** king) for what was once GM's Euclid division. Euclid had to be sold under anti-monopoly laws and was acquired in 1968 by White, who in turn sold it to Mercedes-Benz in 1977.

The other big U.S. car and truck firm, Chrysler, discontinued building anything bigger than medium-weight Dodge trucks at its Warren (Michigan) plant in the mid-1970s. However, until it sold its European interests to Peugeot-Citroën in 1978 it made semi-heavyweights in Britain under the Dodge badge (Commer, also Chrysler-owned, had been discontinued in 1976), and top-weight Barreiros trucks at its Spanish factory at Madrid. Peugeot-Citroën, with

Left Mack's RW Super Liner, its big western-model 6 x 4 tractor. Mack is the last of the American heavy-truck specialists to make its own engines, although for the RW and other heavies big Cummins and Caterpillar units are also available.

Below GMC is the only other U.S. truck firm to make its own engines (Detroit Diesels), although the Astro shown here also uses proprietary units. Chevrolet, GM's other commercial-vehicle subsidiary, no longer builds heavy trucks.

Kenworth, one of the PACCAR group, is largest of the American 'assemblers'. The well-earned reputation for strength of its site vehicles applies also to its big road trucks, of which this mid-1960s conventional tractor is typical.

no stake in the heavy-truck field since before World War II, are anxious to expand their Talbot subsidiary Dodge's share of the market.

When one thinks of the best-known names in heavy-duty trucks worldwide, Mack, White, and Kenworth are sure to come near the top of the list. Mack (founded in 1902) is especially notable in that it is one of the last American specialised builders to be more a manufacturer than an assembler, making its own diesels (although it also offers proprietary makes) as well as many of its own transmission components. The larger Macks use the firm's patented Maxidyne 'constant-torque' diesel engines. Lower down the weight range Scania technology has been employed since the 1940s, while the latest generation of mid-weight Macks are Renaults in disguise, following the French giant's purchase of a 20 per cent stake in the Allentown (Penn.) company.

Mack can perhaps best be likened to MAN or Leyland in Europe, all of whose heavy vehicles are technically very advanced and who also make a high proportion of their own components. Mack makes cab-over and conventional top-weight line-haul trucks, 'specials' including fire-appliance chassis, and various 6 x 4 and 6 x 6 trucks for the construction industry. These last have conventional cabs that are specially offset to the left or right to improve the driver's visibility.

Mack has not had an easy time over the past decade and most of its efforts to expand into new areas have failed. It acquired complete or partial control of Bernard in France, Hayes in Canada, and Brockway in New York, all of which went to the wall, and its efforts to increase sales by taking its revered name lower down the weight range have not been particularly successful.

Kenworth (1923), of Seattle (Washington), another 'assembled' marque, has an image of rugged, no-compromise design and makes both on- and off-highway vehicles — the latter particularly for the logging industry and for heavy oilfield transport, where it is the most

widely used make. Kenworth trucks use Detroit, Caterpillar, and Cummins engines and proprietary transmissions and axles. They are built for lightness with strength and have very simple, traditional cab styling.

Kenworth tractors, especially the top-weight conventionals, are much favoured by American owner-operators for line-haul work. So, too, are the broadly similar Peterbilt trucks from Newark, California, especially on the tough routes of the western and south-western states. Both Kenworth (in 1945) and Peterbilt (in 1958) were acquired by the PACCAR group, which makes about 25,000 trucks a year; it also bought the important earth-moving-machinery and dumptruck maker Dart in 1958, and in 1980, as we have seen, acquired the ailing British premium truck builder Foden.

White is another company that has undergone profound changes over the past few years and whose future has been a subject of speculation. Once a major specialised manufacturer, it is now an assembler, buying in most of its major components. It has also disposed of most of its subsidiaries, including its Hercules engine-making plant, the Diamond-Reo truck division (which has since been reformed in a very small way under new ownership), and the previously mentioned Euclid. It makes a broad range of medium-to-heavy White trucks; has a plant devoted to its custom-built, alloy-chassis Western Star range made primarily for the

Below International Harvester, largest of the American specialised heavy-truck manufacturers, builds its top-of-the-range Transtar as a conventional (as here) and as a cab-over tractor. Top gtw of this model is 54.4 tonnes.

Near right Top-weight trucks need big wreckers to come to their aid after accidents or breakdowns. This White Western Star 4 x 2 is a typical example of the American breed.

Far right Peterbilt trucks come from the same stable as Kenworths, and show it. Their lightweight, very powerful conventional tractors are especially popular with western owner-operators.

western states; and owns Autocar, founded in 1908, which is particularly strong in the construction-truck and heavy-haulage field. All its vehicles exhibit a distinct styling flair and good detail design, but in purely engineering terms they are hard to differentiate from the bulk of other U.S. 'heavy metal'.

Another true manufacturer, rather than assembler, is International Harvester (1907), which makes a very wide range of trucks up to its top-weight Fleetstar, Paystar, and Transtar models, and is the largest of the American specialised builders. It also makes many of its own engines up to about 250 bhp; for its largest trucks Caterpillar, Cummins, and Detroit diesels up to 450 bhp are also available. International is unusual in being one of the very few examples of a non-car maker that produces everything in the commercial field from light pick-ups upwards; it is also renowned worldwide for its agricultural and construction equipment. In recent years it has expanded its truck-making network ever wider: it controls the Canadian ultra-heavyweight custom-truck builder Pacific; it owns British Seddon Atkinson (acquired in 1974); and it has a major Australian subsidiary at Melbourne which imports some models but also makes its own ACCO trucks and the Australian Atkinson cab-over heavy-weight. International has an important financial stake in the

Dutch truck builder DAF and in the Spanish Pegaso, and some of its designs are produced or assembled in various Central and South American countries.

There are literally dozens of smaller American truck assemblers, some of which have been mentioned in previous chapters. One general-purpose heavy-truck maker worthy of note is Freightliner, of Portland (Oregon), which was marketed by White until recently. Freightliner has now established it own sales network, which also handles some Volvo truck models. The Freightliner is very much a typical assembled American truck. It originated in 1938 in a Portland (Oregon) fleet operator's requirement: he made a prototype of the sort of truck he wanted, decided to put it into production, and, as the design evolved, managed to sell several to other hauliers, who decided that it was just what they wanted. The firm was bought by Mercedes-Benz in 1981. Freightliner trucks embody many

Maximum-capacity artic, Japanese style. This is a 38-tonne Mitsubishi Fuso FP model, with all-steel tilt cab, 265 bhp straight-six diesel engine, and a two-range five-speed gearbox. Japanese heavy trucks tend to be smaller than their North American and European counterparts, to suit their congested native roads. Mitsubishi makes everything from light pick-up trucks to heavy dumpers.

lightweight features for which operators have to pay more as extras on competitive models. A similar concept, involving wide use of aluminium and glass-fibre, underlies the high-quality top-weight conventionals and cab-overs built by Marmon, of Garland (Texas).

American Motors Corporation, once the fourth major U.S. car builder, does not make commercial vehicles, although an associate of its Jeep division makes military trucks. Renault, however, bought American Motors in 1980 and may well introduce its own trucks via this convenient outlet in the near future.

Japan and the rest of the world

In contrast to the success of its cars and light trucks in world markets, Japan is only now beginning to make headway with exporting its heavy trucks except in the Far East and Australia. This is partly because in so congested a home country, with tens of thousands of owner-operators of small vans and pickups, there has until recently been little demand for 'heavies' except for specialised purposes. As a result, only in the past few years have the mass-produced car and light-truck manufacturers had ranges extending above the 5 tons gvw class — a situation similar to that in Europe in the 1950s. The four heavy-truck makers, Mitsubishi, Hino, Isuzu, and Nissan Diesel all have car-making connections. Mitsubishi, a broad-based industrial

giant making everything from electrical goods to ships, builds Colt cars (in which Chrysler has an interest) and Fuso heavy trucks. Hino, which traces its origins to TGE, founded in 1917, is owned by Toyota. Isuzu, founded in 1933, has close links with General Motors and, as we have seen, makes many of the heavy trucks sold as Bedfords in Australia. Nissan Diesel is half owned by Nissan (maker of Datsun cars, and part-owner of the Ebro truck of Spain) and half by Minsei Diesel, a builder of diesel-powered trucks since the mid-1930s.

Japanese trucks tend to be smaller and more compact than vehicles for equivalent loads produced elsewhere, and it is doubtful whether they would be allowed to gross their Japanese maximum weight in many European countries or American states even if they complied with local regulations in other ways. By 1981 the only firm to have made any serious sales efforts in Europe was Hino, which sends components to Belgium and Ireland for local assembly and is proposing a similar small-scale operation in Britain. Hino's largest 4 x 2 cab-over model is approved for 32-ton operation in Britain and is offered with a Hino in-line six-cylinder 235 bhp diesel, a Hino V-8 270 bhp diesel, or various Cummins engines.

As a broad generalisation Japanese manufacturers favour V-form engines, make most of their own parts, and have not yet attempted to emulate the new generation of European and American low-unladen-weight, economy-tuned heavyweights. All four firms make a variety of specialised trucks, including crane carriers, crash tenders, and dump trucks; we have already mentioned (Chapter 3) the Tokyo firm of Komatsu, which has been building giant, off-road dumpers since 1953 and Cummins diesel engines since 1961.

Of the remaining countries outside Europe, many have truck-assembly industries but none makes true heavy-weights, except for specialised purposes. China mass-produces medium-weight trucks for its own needs and is planning to produce bigger types; India has Leyland, Bedford, MAN and Mercedes-Benz production plants; Steyr (an Austrian firm), Leyland, Fiat, Mercedes-Benz, and others have assembly plants in various countries of Africa. The Scandinavian firms are strong in South America, which also has the indigenous FNM of Brazil (which uses Fiat designs), DINA, Ramirez, FAMSA (International-based), and Pena; this last makes typical American-style conventional line-haul trucks from components produced by the blossoming Mexican motor-parts industry.

These, then, are the major truck builders of the world. Virtually every other maker is in the specialist field, although firms such as Dennison in Eire, Scot in Canada, and Leader in Australia make normal highway trucks in small numbers (in the case of Dennison, about three per week). The demand for heavy trucks has been seriously affected since the late 1970s by ever more stringent taxation and legislation by the steadily rising price of diesel fuel, and by the world recession. It seems inevitable that it will be companies with the greatest resources behind them that weather the storm; in the meantime several more names are bound to disappear.

In spite of this, some of the smaller firms are in a remarkably fit state because they have become sufficiently flexible to be able to twist and turn with changing market requirements and make some of the most productive trucks. The fact that their vehicles are often more expensive to purchase does not necessarily worry an operator. The initial purchase price of a truck accounts for only about 15 per cent of its total cost over its whole life, and the better the truck the lower is its depreciation and the smaller are the chances of an expensive breakdown.

It will be interesting to see whether the in-house 'manufacturing' or the 'assembly' concept comes to dominate the industry over the next 20 years. In Britain the old-established manufacturer Dennis (famous now as a specialist but once on a par with Leyland for road-haulage trucks) is adopting 'assembly' for its new Delta range, if that is anything to go by. Even firms such as Mercedes-Benz now buy in some major components such as gearboxes, although it is unlikely that they will allow themselves to become dependent on too great a proportion of proprietary parts.

We have had a look at the evolution of the truck, the wide variety of uses to which the top-weight vehicles are put, the various types of specialised and series-production trucks, and the technical background of the modern heavy vehicle. But what about the people for whom trucks are made?

Taking Britain as a fairly typical example of a 'truck-intensive' country, we find that users are broadly divided into haulage companies, specialist buyers such as municipalities, 'own-account' operators (manufacturers who transport their own goods), truck-rental and contract-hire companies, and, not so typically, a state-owned section which includes trucks run by British Rail as well as the general-haulage and rental fleets of British Road Services, plus the specialised fleet of Pickfords used for removals and ultra-heavy haulage.

A high proportion of the heavy trucks that appear in this book are owned by general-haulage contractors, who range from vast firms with hundreds of vehicles down to the smallest unit of all — the owner-driver, comprising one man and one vehicle. Many of the bigger firms offer a distribution and warehousing service which involves collecting goods from customers in maximum-weight trucks, storing them, and then distributing them to shops or other outlets in smaller vehicles — nowadays often vehicles of less than 7.5 tonnes gross, which do not require drivers with HGV (Heavy Goods Vehicle) licences.

In Britain all drivers of vehicles of this weight and above must have such licences, of which there are various classes or grades. The driving examination is much more stringent than the ordinary car-driving test, particularly if a licence to drive artics is required. However, drivers with the top HGV licence are always in great demand.

The trucker's world

A great deal of nonsense has been written in recent years about the supposedly free-and-easy life of the trucker, and a whole mystique has grown up around the 'lonesome-cowboy' image of the long-distance driver, especially in North America. The truth is that truck driving is a demanding and responsible job which suits individualists and those unwilling to be tied by the average nine-to-five job. Nowadays, of course, drivers are not expected to be able to repair and service their trucks, as in bygone days, but they do have the responsibility for spotting tell-tale signs of what, if ignored or unnoticed, might develop into expensive repairs or lead to breakdowns. They have to get to distant and often unfamiliar destinations safely and in good time, they must be able to handle a great deal of paperwork, especially if they are crossing state boundaries in North America or national boundaries in the EEC.

Pages 68-9 The Leyland Roadtrain 16.28 artic for up to 44 tonnes gtw was voted 1981 European Truck of the Year by judges from six countries. This sleeper-cab version has the Leyland TL12 Flexitorque turbo giving 280 bhp, but more power may be offered on models for export to mainland Europe.

Left Typical of the terrain that drivers and vehicles have to cope with on the long and lonely Middle East routes is this mountain pass in Saudi Arabia, seen being negotiated by a

350 bhp Volvo F89 artic. Truck reliability of a high order is a must on routes like this, where spares and breakdown services are few.

Above This highly customised Kenworth conventional, with masses of chromium brightwork and a smart paint job, is obviously owner-operated. The driver sports typical trucker gear of cowboy hat. The big 'West Coast' mirror and vertical exhaust pipe with protective mesh heat shield are characteristic of the heavyweight American rigs.

In Europe they must conform to restrictions on the daily amount of driving that is legally permissible. Nowadays the tachograph (or 'spy in the cab', as it has been unfairly dubbed), which is a sort of combined speedometer and clock, gives a tamper-proof printed record on a card disc of exactly what a truck has been doing. Limited to a maximum eight hours' driving per day and four hours' in any single driving stint, drivers of a heavy vehicle may in future take their enforced rest period in the sleeping compartment of their cab; already many 'night cabs' are fitted with cookers, fridges, and television, and some, particularly in North America and for operation from Europe to the Middle East, are air-conditioned.

In view of the isolation of the typical truck driver it is not surprising to find that the roadstops where he eats, telephones his home or office, or has a shower, are oases of conviviality, where the staff lend a sympathetic ear, and where there are often a billiards (or pool) table, colour television, jukebox, and gaming machines to help while away the evenings away from home. Few would claim that the food served in most truckstops is particularly enterprising, although in its simple way it is often better cooked and fresher than in the average mass-catering restaurant on British motorways.

A noteworthy exception is the Relais Routiers transport restaurant network, mainly in France but with a few supporters in other countries. These are individually owned restaurants which are selected and graded by inspectors. A meal in a typical Routiers may cost £3 or so — which is more than most British drivers are willing to pay — but it is often up to the standard of a good Soho restaurant. Indeed, so excellent but moderately priced is the food that more and more ordinary travellers are willing to make detours to eat in them.

In the United States and mainland Europe truckers communicate with each other by means of Citizen's Band (CB) short-wave radio. The North American and mainland Europe frequency is 27 MHz AM, which offers a range of over 16 km (10 miles). Trucking interests in Britain have strongly advocated 27 MHz for the so-called Open Channel that is going to be given a limited trial in the UK. In fact, the British frequencies are to be 928 MHz AM and 27 MHz FM. Illegally installed 27 MHz AM transmitters in British trucks have already disrupted hospital walkie-talkie systems. On the other hand 928 MHz offers a range of only about 5 km (3 miles) — too short, in the opinion of many truckers; while a switch to 27 MHz FM equipment would be very expensive. Meanwhile, the Carfax channel of the BBC will bring road news to drivers wherever they may be in the UK.

CB, as Open Channel is sure to be known here, seems unlikely to become as much a part of the truckers' way of life in Britain as it has in North America. There a whole new trucker sub-culture has evolved (and been strenuously promoted), with its own radio jargon, its music (a rather feeble form of country-and-western), and even films to glorify it. CB undoubtedly helps to alleviate the monotonous hours spent on dead straight superhighways, and allows friends to keep in touch or important messages to be relayed over great distances via trucks at the outer ends of the transmitter range.

Cab comfort

The modern heavy truck has the brakes and performance to match private car traffic and, if due allowance is made for its extra size and the complexity of its gearbox, it is not much more difficult to drive than a car. Truck drivers often claim to prefer the ride of the refined suspension of a laden truck to that of a car, and anyone would agree that the eye-level view from the cab, 2.75 m (9 ft) above the road, is far superior to anything that car drivers experience.

Until five years ago the standard of comfort and convenience in the average American or British truck fell far below the best that those of mainland Europe were offering. Many of the most successful continental truck makers were (and are) better known to the general public for their cars — Fiat, Mercedes-Benz, Volvo, Saab (Scania), and Daf are examples — and drivers' expectations were higher. The result was that car standards of trim, driving ease, and comfort were built into trucks, while legislation gradually reduced the level of engine noise permissible in the cab to little more than that in the average car.

When Britain joined the EEC, lower tariffs and new upper-weight limits meant that continental trucks flooded into the UK, and their much greater refinement in these respects was often enough to obscure the fact that in terms of engineering, economy, and unladen weight the British trucks were often far superior.

Main picture With up to 4,800 km (3,000 miles) between its Atlantic and Pacific coasts, North America is very much the land of the long-haul trucker. This Kenworth reefer is crossing Salt Lake Flats in Utah on U.S.40, one of the east-west transcontinental routes.

Inset A tachograph is now installed in every long-haul truck operating within the EEC. It is a combined speedometer, clock, and milometer that measures the duration of each journey, the truck speed, the number of stops, and other data, and makes a tamper-proof record on a circular card. Although it is unpopular with many drivers, it offers them protection against unfair accusations of speeding or exceeding driving limits.

The American industry was afflicted in much the same way and was not helped by the sudden swing to economy motoring in the late 1970s, which let in hordes of Japanese cars and light commercial vehicles, and in the truck field gave rise to an insatiable demand for medium-weight diesel trucks (hitherto only the 'heavies' had been diesel powered). Amongst several popular imports, some of which are assembled locally, are Mercedes-Benz, Magirus, SAVIEM/Renault (sold under the Mack name and possibly soon under American Motors), and Volvo (sold through the Freightliner network).

The heavy-truck class in North America — Class 8, which for most interstate rigs means a maximum gross weight of 76,000 lb (34,473 kg) — is dominated by the native United States companies, but there has been a great effort in the past few years to bring driver comfort up to European standards. In cab-temperature control, air-suspension seats, and driving position American trucks are usually at least as good as the Europeans. In addition, the 'conventionals', which account for 40 per cent of top-weight tractors, a far higher proportion than in Europe, have the great advantage of doing away with the 'engine bulge' in the cab, thereby giving more space and avoiding much unwanted noise and heat. The driver also

sits nearer the centre of the wheelbase (except in the case of set-back front-axle designs), and therefore is far less prone to the pitching and vibration which inevitably occur in 'cab-over' designs, where the front axle is directly beneath him. Owing to its 'stepped' profile an American conventional is aerodynamically superior to most slab-fronted cab-overs (it will typically save about ½ cent per mile on this score). On the other hand cab-over tractors can have a shorter wheelbase, and offer extra trailer compatibility and flexibility owing to the stringent limits on the overall lengths of trucks. For this reason, fleet operators generally prefer cab-overs.

Trucking economics

Ask any haulage man and he will tell you that the complexities of running a fleet have multiplied alarmingly in the last few years. Rates chargeable have not kept up with the rocketing prices of fuel and labour, and paperwork has increased drastically. In fact, it has become so complicated that in Britain one person in each fleet has to hold a Certificate of Competence to prove that he is capable of understanding all the rules and regulations which govern the industry. All too often in the past hauliers have been excellent drivers or mechanics but inept businessmen or organisers. This all had to change when plating and testing and other recent requirements came into force. Plating refers to the specification plate that all trucks in Britain and several other countries must now bear to show exactly what weights they were designed (and are permitted) to carry. They are scrupulously tested each year to see that in every respect they are still capable of carrying their designed load safely. Every crucial component is steam cleaned so that a minute inspection can be made; the older the vehicle is, the more likely is it that its plated load capacity will be reduced by the inspectors or that it will be taken off the road because the cost of bringing it up to standard does not make economic sense.

A typical 32-ton tractive unit in Britain in 1981 cost in the region of £30,000 on the road, to which had to be added the cost of the trailer. This represented well over £100 a week in interest charges, and as much or more was taken up by the driver's wages. To this were added depreciation, and maintenance, licensing, and fuel costs. With derv (the acronym is derived from 'diesel-engined road vehicle') at £1.60 per gallon or more and typical consumption of a 32-tonner of around 7 mpg, fuel costs could easily exceed £200 per week. No wonder that trucks must be used intensively to be made to pay their way, and that it is vital that they must be completely reliable.

Many a driver wants something to differentiate his truck from other, similar ones on the road; after all, it is his life, place of work, office, and even home for much of the time. Distinctive fleet liveries help, especially if it is a firm that people enjoy working for and are proud to belong to. The only way a driver's personality can rub off on a vehicle belonging to a large company is a discreet sign giving his name, or some amusing or heartfelt slogan.

The smaller the firm, the more likely its trucks are to be customised; the ultimate expression of the art is usually the owner-driver's truck. Here there is no group livery to be adhered to and the more eye-catching the truck is the more likely it is to attract customers — or at least to make its owner feel distinctive. The most obvious area for customising is the paintwork (some US truckmakers offer customised paint schemes direct from the factory), but trucks are also transformed by the addition of chrome exhaust stacks, roof-mounted lights and trumpet horns, windscreen visors, tinted glass, and countless other modifications to make them more individualistic and comfortable.

International operations

As often as not it is these trucks, by the very nature of their ownership, that become involved in the most risky of all transport undertakings — that of taking goods to places that larger firms would not be geared to fit into their schedule. It is the owner-drivers that keep open many of the routes in the Australian outback that would be uneconomic for bigger firms to operate. In Europe it is often the owner-drivers who carry the loads on the lucrative Middle East run — and face all sorts of difficulties on the way. They really are the new pioneers: once beyond the borders of the EEC and its immediate neighbours, drivers are very much on their own if things go wrong. Visas, customs requirements, and general paperwork are extremely

Saurer, of Arbon in Switzerland, is known for technical innovation — it was a pioneer of diesels in the 1920s, and in the late 1970s it designed and developed a new V-8 unit for Fiat — and for its excellent if expensive trucks and buses. Seen here is a 1981 version of the D290 model, launched in 1977. This model and the similar D330 are both powered by 12-litre, six-cylinder diesels, the more powerful D330 having a greater degree of turbocharging.

complicated (typically, over 30 documents have to be carried), and even obtaining fuel can present difficulties. The worst that can befall a driver is for his truck to break down or be involved in an accident. Many truck makers have no form of representation or repair network outside Europe and, even if they do, spares can sometimes take weeks to obtain. An accident often results in the load and vehicle being impounded and the driver being held in custody until his insurance is proved to be valid. Further wranglings often arise from the documentation and customs clearance for the load.

In an effort to harmonise customs arrangements in Europe the Transportes International des Routiers (TIR) system was evolved. Under this a vehicle could be sealed by the customs in the country where it was loaded and then sent to its destination with the minimum fuss and hindrance, and with duty payable only at the end of its journey. The TIR Convention was formulated in 1959 and the blue and white TIR plates carried on many long-distance vehicles became a familiar sight.

Many countries around the world, including the Soviet Union, Japan, and the USA, are signatories to the convention, which covers EEC vehicles starting or finishing journeys outside the Community. At least 75 per cent of loads carried by EEC-based vehicles remain within the community's borders, so that the TIR is not involved; in these cases, the Community Transit system of documentation somewhat simplifies the passage of goods from one country to another.

To use the TIR system haulers have to obtain **carnets,** books of 14 or 20 pages each made up of double 'tickets'. The smaller book allows up to seven national boundaries to be crossed; the larger allows longer journeys — for example, to the Middle East. Each ticket consists of a manifest of the load and details of the journey; the duplicate is kept by the customs authority at each frontier, while the counterfoil is returning to the issuing authority on the completion of the trip. The issuer is normally the national haulage association in each country, under authority from the United Nations-backed International Road Transport Union (IRU) in Geneva.

The national associations, such as the BDF in Germany, the ATA in the United States, and the RHA (representing hauliers) and FTA (representing own-account operators) in Britain, have to guarantee all **carnets** that they issue and undertake to pay duties, taxes, interest, or fines. To ensure that they do not end up footing the bill, they insist that **carnet** users indemnify them against all forms of loss. Some indivisible loads, such as giant machine tools, are allowed to travel under the TIR convention on flat-bed trucks or trailers, but in general normal loads have to be in customs-approved containers or special bodies sealed by customs authorities.

The way ahead

The future of road haulage depends on many factors, not least its success or otherwise in competing against rival forms of transport, the need to conserve dwindling world stocks of fuel, and the prodigious cost of repairing and maintaining the road networks. As far as road versus rail transport is concerned, the rivalry tends to generate more heat than rational argument. There is no doubt that road transport is more flexible than rail simply because road networks are much more extensive and ramified than railways. By the same token, however, trucks — especially the big ones — are much more of a public nuisance in terms of noise, traffic congestion, and air pollution. Transport legislation is usually likely to favour rail in western Europe, where most of the railways are state-owned, whereas road transport remains largely in the private sector.

By the beginning of 1981 Britain was planning to raise the maximum gcw for trucks from 32 to 44 tons. There was considerable public objection to this on the grounds that the larger trucks would be noisier, would wear out roads quicker, and that the increased vibrations they set up would cause even greater damage to houses, bridges, and other buildings than they do already. Statistics can be made to prove anything, but the British Road Research Laboratory has conducted exhaustive tests that seem to show that the 44-tonners would cause little more damage than the 32-tonners. Nonetheless, the cost of making roads in general suitable for the higher weights will run into hundreds of millions of pounds. On the other hand, there is no reason why the weight per square inch on each tyre should rise, as additional axles could easily be added to help spread the load.

The alternative to this seems to be to have more and lighter trucks, which in themselves would probably cause as much or more damage, as well as require thousands of extra drivers, use more fuel, and add to general road congestion. Already trucks are banned from

Left DAF uses its 11.6-litre straight-six diesel with varying degrees of turbocharging in different versions of its 2800 range. The DKTD gives 248 bhp, the DKS 307 bhp, and the DKSE (an economy version of the DKS) 280 bhp. Full benefits of the economy version demand skilful use of the 16-speed ZF box (13-speed Fuller on UK model) to keep the engine at its most fuel-efficient speed.

Right Volvo Globetrotter vies with the Renault TR305 (pages 18-19) as Europe's most luxurious long-haul express. It is basically the top-weight F12 tractor with (for some markets) an after-cooled turbo diesel giving 385 bhp and a raised cab roof that enables the crew to stand up. The cab offers masses of storage space above the windscreen and under the lower of the two bunks (where the fridge is also located), and a cooker and sink above the engine cover. Air-conditioning and tinted glass are both standard features.

many mainland Europe roads on Sunday, and more and more secondary roads are permanently barred to them. There is a strong trend for Europe to follow North America and confine its heavy trucks to a few purpose-built superhighways or motorways, with distribution terminals at various points along them like railway goods yards for transferring loads to smaller, local-delivery vehicles. In North America two trailers can be hauled on this sort of trunking work, while in Australia there are few restrictions and road trains can consist of even more cumbersome outfits, especially on the straight, flat roads of the outback.

The status of the heavy-truck driver has improved immensely since the 1950s. Then he was expected to drive a vehicle with heavy and difficult controls that was hard-pushed to keep up a 35 km/h (22 mph) average on British roads, owing to the very low power output of contemporary engines (110 to 150 bhp was deemed adequate for a 24-ton gross-weight truck, and gearboxes had far fewer ratios than today). Cabs were cramped and draughty and heaters were very

much an optional extra that was rarely specified by penny-pinching fleet operators. Loading was mostly by hand, so drivers had to wear rough clothes, which did little to enhance the public image of the driver or his industry.

Contrast all that with today's super-efficient and powerful trucks, with 400 bhp or more at their disposal, power-assisted steering and brakes, and a variety of mechanical aids for loading and unloading. Small wonder that many of today's drivers wear smart working clothes and look like executives — which indeed they are in terms of their responsibility for load and vehicle while out on the road or delivering to a customer.

In mainland Europe this new image is reflected in special radio programmes for truckers which go out every night. Most of them spend a great deal of time publicising the social benefits of trucks and trucking, conducting phone conversations with drivers, tracing stolen loads, aiding crash victims, and promoting the growing truckers' fraternity around the world.

GLOSSARY

After-cooling In turbocharging, a method by which the air, having been compressed, and so heated, is cooled before it enters the combustion chamber. Cooling increases the air's density, and so increases power output and improves combustion efficiency.

Artic An articulated truck, consisting of a tractor and a semi-trailer. The truck articulates (pivots) about the fifth wheel.

BBC Bumper-to-back-of-cab measurement on truck cabs. Most countries have truck-length limits; the shorter the cab, the longer can be the semi-trailer or payload part of the truck.

Bhp Brake-horsepower, the maximum power that an engine develops (at a given rpm); the figure quoted for an engine varies according to which measuring standard (SAE, DIN, etc) is used. *See also* kW.

Bogie An assembly of two or more axles.

Cab-over-engine *see* Forward control.

CB Citizen's Band radio.

COE *see* Forward control.

Constant mesh Describes a gearbox in which the gear wheels on the output shaft are permanently meshed with their counterparts on the layshaft. Those on the output shaft can spin freely until selection of a gear locks the relevant gear wheel to the shaft.

Container A freight container of a standard size used in international road, rail, and sea traffic. Those used in the EEC are in three lengths, 12.19 m (40 ft), 9.13 m (29 ft 11¼ in), and 6.06 m (19 ft 10½ in); two heights, 2.44 m (8 ft) and 2.59 m (8 ft 6 in); and one width, 2.44 m (8 ft).

Conventional *see* Normal control.

Derv Diesel-engined-road-vehicle: the British acronym for diesel-engine fuel; in North America the fuel is known simply as 'diesel'.

Down-time Any period during which a commercial vehicle is not earning income, as during repairs or servicing.

Drawbar trailer A trailer drawn by a rigid or artic.

Eighteen-wheeler In American parlance, any artic; strictly, an artic consisting of a three axle tractor and a two-axle semi-trailer.

Eight-legger A four-axle, eight-wheel rigid truck, with four steerable front wheels. A common design for on/off-road dumpers, especially in Britain.

Fifth wheel The coupling on an artic tractor for a semi-trailer. It consists of a heavy, flat steel plate with a hole in the centre into which a vertical pin on the semi is slotted.

Flitch Plate-steel local reinforcement of a chassis member.

Forward control Design of a tractor or rigid truck in which the cab is mounted over, rather than behind, the engine. In North America the style is called cab-over-engine, usually shortened to COE or cab-over. Most forward-control cabs can be tipped forward to an angle of 60 degrees or more, allowing access to the engine from the rear.

Gcw Gross combined weight — the maximum permitted weight of an artic tractor and its loaded semi-trailer.

Glider kit Replacement 'half-truck' (engine, front end of chassis, and cab) offered by several North American truck builders to extend the life of worn-out vehicles.

GRP Glass-reinforced plastic, used by some truck builders for cab and, especially, engine-bonnet panels.

Gtw Gross train weight — the maximum permitted weight of a towing vehicle and its trailer(s) when loaded.

Gvw Gross vehicle weight — the maximum permitted weight of a vehicle when loaded.

Half-cab A cab occupying half (or less) of the width of a truck and mounted centrally or on one side of the chassis. Found mainly on off-road vehicles.

HGV Heavy goods vehicle. In Britain HGVs are divided into various classes according to weight and whether rigid or articulated, and the various grades of HGV driving licences correspond to these classes.

Inter-cooling *see* After-cooling.

Jack-knife An accident, usually caused by a slippery road surface, in which an artic goes out of control and the tractor and/or semi slew round toward each other.

kW Kilowatt; used as an alternative unit to brake-horsepower, especially in mainland Europe. 1 kW = 1,000 Watts = 1·34 bhp; 1 bhp = 746 Watts.

Landing gear The front parking wheels (usually retractable) of a semi-trailer.

LPG Liquefied petroleum gas, a propane or propane-butane fuel that can be used as an alternative to petrol.

Normal control Design of tractor or rigid truck in which the cab is behind the engine and its bonnet. In North America it is called 'conventional'.

Open Channel The British equivalent of Citizen's Band radio. British frequencies (1981) are 928 MHz AM and 27 MHz FM.

Plating Refers to the specification plate on heavy trucks in Britain. Renewed annually, it displays the maximum payload the truck is permitted to bear.

PSV Public service vehicle, such as an omnibus.

Range change In a gearbox, a system in which each gear has more than one ratio.

Reefer A refrigerated truck, trailer, or semi.

Retarders Engine- or exhaust-powered systems for reducing road speed, independent of the service brakes.

Rigid A non-articulated truck — as, for instance, an eight-legger.

Rough-neck Informal name for a large, all-wheel-drive self-loading truck for off-road (typically desert) operation.

Self-loader A truck equipped with its own mechanical loading device such as a crane or winch.

Semi-trailer A trailer, with no front axle, that is coupled to a tractor, as with most articulated trucks.

Skeletal A virtually bodyless rigid truck or trailer designed to carry a detachable container.

Sleeper A cab with sleeping accommodation.

SMC Sheet-moulding compound, a plastic material used in the panels of truck cabs.

Splitter A unit for 'splitting' gears into high and low ratios; usually mounted on the front of the gearbox.

Tachograph A mechanical driver's log that provides a tamper-proof record of truck speed, mileage, and duration of journey.

Tag axle A removable axle fitted to the back of a truck to increase permissible payload where individual axle loadings are critical. Much used in the United States, where maximum permitted axle loadings vary from state to state.

Tandem Two axles mounted as a pair.

TIR Transportes International des Routiers, the system of custom arrangements governing the use of sealed trucks and trailers between EEC and neighbouring countries.

Torque Twisting effort. An engine's torque rating indicates the usable power available at the crankshaft at optimum engine speed. Torque is expressed in Newton-metres or pounds-feet. 1 Nm = 0 74 lb f. ft; 1 lb f. = 1·36 Nm.

Torque converter In transmission, an alternative to a clutch in which power from the crankshaft is transmitted to the gearbox input shaft by means of a fluid coupling. Torque converters are used mainly in conjunction with automatic gearboxes.

Torque rise Used of a turbocharged engine developing near-maximum torque over a wide rev. band, usually at low engine speeds.

Tri-axle A semi-trailer with three close-coupled axles.

Turbocharger A system of compressor and pump that forces air under pressure into an engine's combustion chambers. Whereas a turbocharger is driven by the engine's exhaust gases and its speed is generally governed by the temperature of those gases, the more old-fashioned supercharger is driven (usually by a belt) by the engine itself, and so creams off some engine power.

Wrecker Informal North American name for a large breakdown or truck-recovery vehicle.

A 1981 Marmon HDT long-haul cab-over tractor; a conventional, the CHDT, is also made. Marmon is a small firm which is able to make its way in a formidably competitive field by carrying customisation to a point where each buyer can specify what is virtually a unique vehicle. The tractors are available in 4 x 2 and 6 x 4 forms, most proprietary makes of diesel from 335 to 450 bhp can be ordered, and cabs of various BBCs are offered, including this extra-long night cab.

INDEX

Numbers in **bold** type refer to captions

AEC (Associated Equipment Co) 10, 11, 56
Aerodynamics 45
After-cooling 36, **37**, **39**, 78
Albion 9, 56
Allison (GM) transmissions **26**, 28, 42, 43
All-wheel-drive trucks 27, 33
American LaFrance **26**, 27
American Motors Corporation 67
Astra 28
Autocar 9, 31, 43, 66; Construcktor 2 40; 6 x 4 30
Aveling-Barford 28, 56
Axle arrangements 20-1

Baribbi (fire equipment) **26**
Barreiros 49, 61
Bedford 12, 30, 38; 4 x 4 33; TK 19; TL 19; TM **5**, 39, 54
BELAZ 28, 59
Benz 8, 11
Benz, Karl 8
Berliet 16, 36, 44, 50, **54**; TR 280 **50**; TR305 18
Berna 49
Bollée, Amédée 8
Bollnas 30
Braking systems 43
Brewery vehicles 30

Cabs 16-20; comfort in 72, 74; tilting 12, 19
Carmichael (fire equipment) 27
Caterpillar 28, 36, 38, 39, 61; 3406 **28**; 3408 40
CCC (Crane Carrier Co) 30; 6 x 6 33
Chassis 43; automatic lubrication 45
Chevrolet 10, 43, 61; Titan 43
Chrysler 61
Chubb (fire equipment) 27
Chuting Star 6 x 6 33
Citroën 10, 50. See also Peugeot-Citroën
Clark transmissions 42
Cline 28
Club of Four: see ETD
Coder (trailers) 21
Coleman 30
Commer 9, 10, 38, 61
Consolidated Dynamics 30
Containerization 21
Cranes, mobile 30
Crash tenders 27
Crown Firecoach (fire equipment) 27
Cummins engines 11, **16**, **26**, 36, 37, 38-9, **56**, **61**; NT 240 **37**
'Curtain siders' 22, 23
CVS 30; 6 x 6 33

DAF (Van Doornes Automobielfabrieken) 16, 30, 49, 51, 52, **54**, 66; FT 2300 **53**; FT 2800 **76**
DAF engines: DK series **76**
Daimler, Gottlieb 8
Dana transmissions 42
Dart 28, 56, 64
De Dion, Bouton 8
Dennis 9, 16, 27, 30, 67; Delta range 67;
Dennison 16, 67
Derv 78
Detroit Diesel engines **26**, **28**, 33, 37-8, 61; 8V-92T **39**
Deutz engines 38, 39, 49; BF8L 413F **39**
Diesel, Rudolf 10-11
Diesel engines 10-11
DINA (Diesel Nacional) 67
DJB 29
Dock trucks 30-1
Dodge 10, 12, 49, 61-2
Douglas 30, 33
Dump trucks 28-9
Duplex 27, 33

Eaton transmissions 42
Ebro 39, 49
Electric vehicles 8-9, 40
Engine designs 36-40
ERF (E.R. Foden) 10, 19, 36, 38, 56; B-series 18, 56
ETD (European Truck Development or Club of Four) 16, 49, 50
Euclid 28, 50, 61
Extra-heavy haulage vehicles 31

Fabco WT 6 x 6 33
FAMSA 67
Faun **26**, 27, 28, 30, 50; 8 x 8 33
FBW (Franz Brozincevic, Wetzikon) 39, 49
Fiat 39, 49, 52, **75**; 190F 35, **49**
Fifth wheel 78
Fire engines 27, 40
Flextruck 6 x 6 33
FMC (fire equipment) 27
FNM (Fabrica Nacional de Motores) 67
Foden 8, 12, 16, 18, 19, 38, 45, 54, 56, 64; Fleetmaster 54; Haulmaster 54, **59**; 6 x 6 33; steam wagon **8**
Ford (Europe) 30, 39, 54; Transcontinental 16, 42, 50, 54, **56**, 61
Ford (USA) 10, 12, 38, 59, 61; Model A (1927) 10
Freightliner 66. See also White
Fruehauf Corporation (trailers) 21, **33**
FTF (Floors Handel & Industrie) 16, 51
Fuller Road Ranger (transmission) 42, 76
Fuso 22, **66**, 67. See also Mitsubishi
FWD (Four Wheel Drive Auto Co) 27, 33

Gardner engines 11, 39, **59**
Gas-turbine engines 40
GAZ 59
Gearboxes 42-3
Glider kit 78
GMC (General Motors Truck and Coach Division) 10, 12, 37, 38, 40, 54, 61; Bison 16
Guy 16, 56

Hahn 27
Hanomag-Henschel 50
Harbour trucks 30-1
Hawker-Siddeley 22, 39
Heathfield 28
Hendrickson 27
Hewitt 10
Hewitt, Edward 10
Hino (Toyota) 67

Ibex 30
Inter-cooling: see After-cooling
International Harvester 8, 9, **12**, 49, 51, 54, 66; Fleetstar 66; Paystar 66; 6 x 6 33; Transtar 64, 66
Isuzu 61, 67
IVECO (Industrial Vehicles Corporation) 16, 49

Jelcz 16, 59

Kaelble 27, 28, 50
KAMAZ 6 x 4 59
Kässbohrer (trailers) 21
Kenworth **5**, **8**, 31, 56, 62, 63-4, 71, 72; 6 x 6 33
King Truck Equipment (trailers) 21
Komatsu 28, 67
KRAZ dump trucks 59
Krupp 38

Lancia 33, 49
Lectra Haul 28
Ledwinka, Hans 59
Leyland 9, 11, 18, 30, 36, 38, 39, 40, 51, **54**, 56; Beaver TSC9 11; Constructor 30.21 18, **37**, **43**, 44, 56; Marathon 56; Mastiff 56; 16.28 **37**, 44, 71; T45 Roadtrain 18, **37**, 45, 56

Leyland engines: TL11A **37**; T12 Flexitorque **37**, 71;
LIAZ 59
Licences, HGV 70

Mack 9, 10, 11, 30, 36, 38, 62-3; AC 9; fire engines 27; Maxidyne engines 37, 62; RW Super Liner 6 x 4 61
Magirus-Deutz 16, 27, 33, 49, 50, 54
MAN (Maschinenfabrik Augsburg-Nürnberg) 11, 16, 36, 39, 40, 44, 50, 51, **53**, **54**, **59**; 8 x 8 33; Jumbo 31; 19.240 **21**; 19.321 45
M & G Trailers 21
Marmon 33, 67; HDT **79**
Massey-Ferguson 49
Master Truck 30
Maudslay 9
Maxim 27
MAZ 38, 59
Mercedes-Benz 11, 27, 28, 36, 39, 42, 50-1, 61, 67; all-wheel-drive vehicles 33; 'New Generation' cab 45, 50
Minsei Diesel 67
Mitsubishi 30, **66**, 67. See also Fuso
Mol 21, 30; 6 x 6 33
Motor Panels (cabs) 16, 18
Mowag 49
Moxy 29
MTU engines 50
MWM (Motorenwerke Mannheim) engines 39

Nissan Diesel 49, 67
Nuova OMT (trailers) 21

ÖAF (Österreichische Automobilfabrik) 16, 51, Jumbo 31, 51
OM (Officine Meccaniche) 49
Oshkosh **26**, 27, 33; B-series **33**; extra-heavy haulage vehicles 31
Ottawa **5**, 30

PACCAR group 56, **59**, **62**, 64
Pacific 31, 66; 6 x 6 33
Panhard et Levassor 8
Pegaso 49, 66
Pena 67
Perkins engines 39
Perlini **26**, 27
Peterbilt **5**, **8**, 56, 64; 6 x 4 **22**
Peter Pirsch 27
Petter (refrigeration units) 22
Peugeot 8
Peugeot-Citroën 12, 49, 61-2
Pierce 27
Primrose 30
Purrey 9

Rába 16, 59
Range change (transmission) **21**, 42, 78
'Reefers' (refrigerated trailers) 22, 78
Refuse-collection trucks 30
Reliance-Mercury 30
Renault 50, 63, 67; TR305 **18**, **76**
Reo 9
Retarders, engine 78
Reynolds-Boughton 27
RFW 27
Ricardo, Sir Harry 11
Rimpull 28
Rockwell 22
Rolls-Royce engines 36, 39, 40, 51; Eagle 200 Mk III **37**
Roman 16, 59
'Roo bar' **50**
'Ro-ro' (roll-on, roll-off) tractor 30

Sandbach Engineering (Foden company) 59
Sankey 18
Saurer 11, 33, 49; D290 **75**; D330 **75**; 5DF 30
SAVIEM (Société Anonyme de Véhicules Industriels et d'Équipements Mécaniques) 16, 49, 50
Scammell 21; 33; 38; 56;

Commander 31, 39; Contractor 16, 31; Nubian 27
Scania 18, 33, 42, 51-2, 62; LB141 **21**, 59
Scot 67
SD (Shelvoke and Drewry) 16, 27, 30
Seagrave 27
Seddon 10, 54
Seddon Atkinson 18, 19, 30, 36, 38-9, 54, 66; 401 **54**
Self-loading trailers 22
Sentinel 8, 39
Sisu 16, 51
Skip loaders 22
SMC (sheet-moulding compound) 16, 18
Snowploughs 33
Spartan 27
Steam-driven vehicles 8
Steering, power 45
Steyr 50, 67
Stuart, Herbert Akroyd 10
Suspension 28, 43-5

Tachograph 71, **72**, 78
TAM (Tovarna Automobilov Maribor) 59
Tankers 22
Tasker (trailers) 21
Tatra 38, 44, 59; 8 x 8 33; 6 x 6 33
Terex 28, 61
Thermo King (refrigeration units) 22
Thornycroft 9, 27, 56; Nubian 27
TIR (Transportes International des Routiers) system 76
Titan 30, 31

Torque converters 42-3
Trailers 21-3
Transmission 42-3
Turbocharging 12, 36, **37**, **39**, 45, 53, 56, 71, 75, 77, 78

Unic 49
Unipower 27
Unit Rig 28

Van Hool (trailers) 21
V-Con 28; Model 3006 29
Volvo 12, 16, 18, 21, 37, 42, 49, 51-2; F7/10/12 36, 52; F85/6/8 52, **59**, 71, F12 Globe trotter 52, 76; N10 33 6 x 4 **54**
Volvo-BM 29

WABCO (Westinghouse Air Brake Co) 28; 3200B Haulpak 28
Walter 27, 33
Ward LaFrance 27
Werklust 29
'West Coast' mirror 71
White 8, 9, 61, 62, 64, 67; Freightliner 40; Road Commander 18; Western Star 28, 49, 64
Willème 12, 31
Wind deflector 45
Wrecker 64, 79

York (trailers) 21

Zastava 59
ZF (Zahnradfabrik Friedrichshafen transmissions 42, 43, 76
ZIL (Zavod Imieni Likhacheva) 59

Acknowledgements

The publishers thank the following for their kind permission to reproduce the pictures in this book:

American LaFrance 26; Nick Baldwin 10, 11, 12, 13, 14-15, 18 above left, 20, 21, 24-5, 26-7 above, 30, 42, 50-1, 53 above, 54, 58-9, 61 below, 65 above left, 74-5; Bedford Commercial Vehicles 2-3, 38; Cummins Engine Co 36 left; DAF Trucks 76; Ian Dawson 55; Deutz Engines 39; Robert Estall 4-5, 28-9, 46-7, Fabco Division, Kelsey-Hayes Co 33; Fiat SpA 48-9; Ford Motor Co 16-17; 56-7; Leyland Vehicles 18 below left, 34-5, 37, 43, 44-5, 45 left, 68-9; Lucas Kienzle Instruments 72 inset; Mack Trucks 9, 36 right, 60-1; MAN AG 45 right; Marmon Motor Co 78-9; Fuso, Mitsubishi Motors 22-3, 66-7; Andrew Morland endpapers 1, 6-7, 22, 41, 62-3, 64-5, 65 above right, 71 above right, 72-3; National Motor Museum 8; Oshkosh Truck Corp 26-7 below; Régie Nationale des Usines Renault 18-19; Volvo Trucks (Great Britain) 77, WABCO 28 inset; White Motor Corp 30-1, 40; Zefa Picture Library (John S. Adams) 52-3, (Bob Croxford) 70-1.

The Author thanks G.N. Georgano, Arthur Ingram, and Martin Phippard for help with the illustrations; R.M. Castle of the FTA for information on truck operation in the EEC; and John Aldridge of Motor Transport, Martin Hayes of Leyland, Phil Reed of Cummins Engine Co, and Graham Sellors of Truck for general advice.

PDO 81-124